Annie Russell Wall

Sordello's Story Retold In Prose

Annie Russell Wall

Sordello's Story Retold In Prose

ISBN/EAN: 9783744652254

Printed in Europe, USA, Canada, Australia, Japan

Cover: Foto ©ninafisch / pixelio.de

More available books at **www.hansebooks.com**

Browning — Works critical

REESE LIBRARY

OF THE

UNIVERSITY OF CALIFORNIA.

Received April, 1891

Accessions No. 43261 *Shelf No.* 95-3
W18

SORDELLO'S STORY

RETOLD IN PROSE

BY

ANNIE WALL

BOSTON AND NEW YORK
HOUGHTON, MIFFLIN AND COMPANY
The Riverside Press, Cambridge
1886

Copyright, 1886,
By ANNIE WALL.

All rights reserved.

43261

The Riverside Press, Cambridge:
Electrotyped and Printed by H. O. Houghton & Co.

To
MY FRIENDS OF THE "SORDELLO CLUB"
This Little Book
IS AFFECTIONATELY DEDICATED
IN MEMORY OF
THE PLEASANT HOURS WHEN WE HEARD
SORDELLO'S STORY
TOLD.

> Ma vedi là un anima, ch' a posta
>   Sola soletta verso noi riguarda;
>   Quella ne insegnerà la via più tosta.
> Venimmo a lei, O anima lombarda,
>   Come ti stavi altera e disdegnosa,
>   E nel muover degli occhi onesta e tarda ?
> Ella non ci diceva alcuna cosa;
>   Ma lasciavane gir, solo guardando,
>   A guisa di leon, quando, si posa.
> Pur Virgilio si trasse a lei pregando
>   Che ne mostrasse la miglior salita;
>   E quella non rispose al suo dimando;
> Ma di nostro paese, e della vita
>   Ci chiese. E 'l dolce Duca incominciava;
>   Mantova. E l' ombra, tutta in sè romita,
> Surse ver lui del luogo ove pria stava,
>   Dicendo; O Mantovano, io son Sordello,
>   Della tua terra. E l' un l' altro abbraciava.
>   DANTE, *Purgatorio*, Canto vi., verses 58-75.

HISTORICAL INTRODUCTION.

Soleva Roma, che 'l buon mondo feo,
   Due Soli aver; che l' una e l' altra strada
   Facean vedere e del Mondo, e del Dio.
L' un l' altro ha spento, ed è giunta la spada
   Col pastorale; e l' un col altro insieme
   Per viva forza mal convien che vada;
Perocchè, giunti l' un l' altro non teme.
   DANTE, *Purgatorio*, Canto 17, Verses 106–112.

HISTORICAL INTRODUCTION.

THE scene of "Sordello" is laid in Lombardy, in the early part of the thirteenth century, when Frederick II. is Emperor, and Honorius III. Pope.

It is needful that we should have some knowledge of the political and social condition of Italy at that period, if we wish to enter into the spirit of the poem, to enjoy its historical allusions or be able in any way to comprehend the problems that vexed Sordello's soul.

The empire of Charles the Great, which he ruled, as he believed, by divine commission, had included nearly all of western Christendom, but the revived empire of Otto the Great, established early in the tenth century, consisted of Germany and Lombardy, with the Romagna, and to this Burgundy was afterwards added; and it was Otto who fixed the principle that to the German king belonged the Roman crown.

The friend and protector of the church, Charles had always held himself the Pope's superior, and Otto and his immediate successors gained many privileges in respect to papal elections.

The crown of Germany was elective, although often passing in one family for several generations, and to the elected King of the Franks, as he was called, came of right, it was understood, the crowns of Burgundy, Lombardy and the Roman Empire, the latter bestowed by the Pope at Rome.

Pope and Emperor were supposed to be the vicars of God on earth in spiritual and temporal affairs, equal and coördinate. But the theory was rarely observed in practice, and the culmination of the struggle for supremacy between the two powers took place in the reign of the Emperor Henry IV. of Franconia, and the papacy of Gregory VII., the famous Hildebrand.

Historical Introduction.

It was the struggle between church and state, which had already occurred on a smaller scale in various cases, and which shortly after broke out in England in the dispute between Henry II. and Becket.

The quarrel ended in a compromise, in which most of the gains were on the side of the papacy, and it was renewed with great fierceness in the reign of Frederick I. of Hohenstaufen, called the Red Beard, who came to the throne in 1152, and who, desiring to vindicate the claims of his office to equal sanctity with that of his opponent, bestowed upon the Empire the title of *The Holy*.

The cities of Lombardy, commonwealths somewhat after the fashion of those of ancient Greece, had grown to be very rich and strong, and although ready to admit the Emperor's authority in theory, were strikingly averse to submitting to any manifestation of it in practice. The city of Milan, by her attacks upon a weaker neighbor, who appealed to Frederick for aid, began a war which resulted in the Peace of Constance in

1183, by which the Cæsar abandoned all but a nominal authority over the Lombard League, which in the long contest had received aid from the Pope, and hence, although some of the cities were strongly imperialist, was mainly papal in its sympathies. The son and successor of Frederick, Henry VI., married Constance, the heiress of the Norman kingdom of Sicily, which was a fief of the papal crown, and thenceforth a new point of quarrel between Pope and Emperor.

On the death of Henry came his brother, Philip, who, being shortly afterwards murdered, made way for Otto of Saxony, a nephew of John of England. But trouble arising between Otto and the Pope, he was finally deposed, and his place filled by Frederick, the son of Henry VI. and Constance of Sicily, who had been chosen, during his father's lifetime, King of the Romans, but was set aside, as too young to govern, in behalf of his uncle, Philip, and, curiously enough, considering his future relations to the papacy, was, in his early years, the ward of Innocent III.

Frederick, *stupor mundi et immutator mirabilis*, as Matthew Paris calls him, received the German crown at Aachen in 1215, the imperial crown at Rome in 1230, and died in 1250 at Fiorentino, worn out with perpetual struggles and under the ban of the Pope. When young he had assumed the cross, and the Church thereby acquired a hold over him which was never abandoned, while disputes in reference to Sicily soon arose between him and Honorius.

When tidings came of the misfortunes which had befallen the French crusaders in Egypt and the loss of Damietta, — mishaps really due to the bad conduct of the crusaders themselves, — the Pope attributed them to Frederick's failure to fulfil his vow. The exigencies of the time, however, seemed to require the Emperor's presence at home, nor was the crusading spirit then especially prevalent in Europe.

John of Brienne, the dethroned king of

Jerusalem, wandered from court to court, vainly seeking aid to recover his crown, and in 1235, Frederick, who had married his daughter, Jolande, declared her claims to be better than her father's, which were asserted only in right of his late wife. He then assumed for himself, in virtue of Jolande's heirship, the title of king, and soon after began to fit out an expedition for the recovery of the kingdom.

In the midst of all these disturbances Honorius died, and his place was filled by a man of great ability, the aged Cardinal Ugolino, who assumed the title of Gregory IX., and issued a mandate to the princes of Christendom for an immediate crusade.

Frederick assembled a fleet at Brindisi, where the plague fell upon his army, cutting off many, among others the Landgrave of Thuringia, the husband of St. Elizabeth of Hungary.

The squadron set sail, but the Emperor falling ill himself, his return was unavoidable, though it brought down a speedy excommunication upon his head; he issued, in reply, an address to the sovereigns of Europe, in which he stated his reasons for returning, and called upon all to resist the intolerable assumptions of the papacy. "Your own houses," wrote he, "are in danger, when your neighbor's is in flames!"

Again excommunicated, Frederick set forth at last, with a fleet of some twenty sail, "more like a pirate than a prince," said Gregory, and landed at Ptolemais, where he was coldly received by the various parties, who, for the moment, hushed their constant bickerings to insult the temporal head of Christendom.

The Sultan of Babylon (Cairo), Malek Kameel, was engaged at that moment in a quarrel with Malek Moadhim, the Sultan of Damascus, and was disposed to give some privileges to the Christians if he could thereby weaken his enemy. He accordingly treated with Frederick for Jerusalem and the surrounding territory, which were to pass into the hands of the Christians, while civil rights and the exclusive possession of the Mosque of Omar were secured to the Moslems. But the Holy City itself was placed under the ban of the Church, and the Patriarch refusing to perform the coronation ceremony, Frederick set the crown upon his head with his own hand, afterwards placing a second diadem upon the brow of his wife.

It was a bloodless triumph, but it drew down upon the victor a storm of reproach, as if never before had treaties been made between Christian and Mohammedan princes; papal intrigues hastened his return, nor did the quarrel end until the death of Gregory.

In an evil hour for Frederick the choice of a new Pope fell upon a Genoese cardinal, upon whom he had conferred many favors, and who, up to this time, had been one of his staunch supporters. "In the Cardinal," said Frederick, to some one who congratulated him on the election, "I have lost my best friend; in the Pope I shall find my worst enemy. No Pope can be a Ghibelline."

Historical Introduction.

In a council summoned in 1245 at Lyons, the Pope, Innocent IV., who found the general sentiment of Europe among princes and people, and even largely among Churchmen, to be opposed to him, proposed to try his case against Frederick.

But the Emperor's lawyer found that no justice was to be looked for, and in an able speech he appealed from that to a future tribunal, from the Pope, who was his sovereign's enemy, to one more just hereafter. Vainly did French and English envoys remonstrate, for even the pious St. Louis and the priest-ridden Henry III. disapproved of Innocent's conduct, the Pope was resolved upon his course.

Without taking the vote of the Council he rose from his seat in the midst of the panic-stricken Churchmen, and declared the Emperor to be excommunicated and deposed, and his subjects absolved from their allegiance, the sentence being accompanied by the extinction of torches and other ceremonial, " while the general awe was heightened by the appearance of a meteor, which, as the words were spoken, shot across the sky."

At this juncture Frederick made the mistake of confounding the cause of the Pope, then everywhere unpopular, with that of the clergy at large; he lost his self-control and indulged in vituperations of the whole body, which caused many of his strongest supporters, the German prelates, to fall away from him, and rendered his cause less generally favored.

Five years of warfare ensued, and in 1250 Frederick expired, in the arms of his son Manfred, who succeeded him in Sicily, leaving behind him a fame which not even papal hatred could destroy.

In Germany, the great Churchmen were long on his side, and when they fell away, his barons, many of them old enemies, rallied about him. His legislation was far in advance of any other of his time, and in some respects, in regard to agriculture and commerce, appears to have anticipated the most advanced thought of to-day; in Sicily he liberated the Commons from the tyranny of feudal lords and ecclesiastical rule, freed the serfs upon his own estates, and legalized ownership of property by that class; made justice easily accessible to all, established semi-annual parliaments where the cities appeared by their delegates, entered into commercial treaties with the great sea-faring nations of the day, and, like Elizabeth of England, engaged in many ventures on his own account.

He founded schools and universities, and Greek being then the spoken language of a large part of his people, its literature was carefully preserved, and might never have passed from the knowledge of Europe, had the rule of his house continued in Sicily.

His knowledge of Arabic opened to him many famous works, and he ordered many translations to be made from that language and the Greek for the use of his subjects, that of Aristotle being intrusted to one of his chief advisers, a scholar from a far-off northern land, "the wizard," Michael Scott. Literature and Art could not fail to flourish under a prince who was himself philosopher and poet; Greek and Arabian writers thronged his court, the Minnesaenger of Germany, the Troubadours of Provence and Guienne, and the French Trouvères wandered over the Alps to join their brethren in minstrelsy, and the Italian Muse sang her first songs in the sweet Sicilian tongue.

Spite of a professed acceptance of the doctrines current in his time, Frederick II. was accounted as being far from orthodox in his religious opinions. His sarcastic wit often shocked an age peculiarly reverential of forms, and his tolerance of the beliefs of others could then be explained only on the supposition that he had lost his own. Moreover, the irregularities of his private life and his occasional outbursts of cruelty laid him open to deserved censure. It is not strange that his faith in church doctrines should have been weakened by the cruel injustice which he suffered from the Church's head, and we can easily believe that a man of his intellectual powers might have glimpses of something better than the average theology of the day; it is quite certain also that most rulers of that period resembled him far more in his defects than in his excellences, and that his ruined life was an irreparable misfortune to Europe.

The strife in the reign of Frederick II. was not, says Dean Milman, "for any specific point in dispute, like the right of investiture, but avowedly for supremacy on one side, which hardly deigned to call itself independence; for independence on the other, which, remotely at least, aspired after supremacy. Cæsar would bear no superior, the successor of St. Peter no equal." [1]

Too far in advance of his age to be in sympathy with it, prevented by force of circumstances from pursuing a consistent imperial policy, Frederick, the wonder of the world though he was, failed to produce

[1] It was a saying in Rome that Cæsar would brook no superior, Pompey no equal.

upon his time any impression commensurate with his vast abilities; yet he did much, and the fruits of his legislation in Germany were reaped in a later reign, while untold prosperity might have been the result in Sicily, but for the French invasion and the ensuing wars.

As for Frederick himself, he remains for us one of the most brilliant and interesting actors upon the stage of the world's history, the most splendid figure in the most splendid of imperial houses, a man whose faults were largely due to his position and the time in which he lived, whose virtues and transcendent powers were all his own.

Nothing could well have been more stormy than life in a mediæval Italian city, where an hundred questions complicated politics in a most perplexing fashion. There were Ghibelline cities, or those that sided with the Emperor in his perennial quarrel with the Pope, and Guelfic cities, or those which supported the Papal cause, but in each was to be found a minority of the opposite party. Every city, moreover, had her ever-recurring disputes with the baron most influential in her territory, while the great burgher-families mingled party politics with private feuds. The strife was waged with horrible cruelty; burning houses, murdered men, women and children were no rare sights in those days; good faith was rare, and treaties seemed made but to be broken. The cities, which were commonwealths much after the old Greek type, had grown rapidly in wealth and power, due largely to the development of the industrial arts, but their literature was, as yet, of foreign growth, and the fine arts were awaiting that full glory that was to come from the flood of Hellenic light that was to waken them to new and diviner life and splendors.

In the eleventh and twelfth centuries there had been developed a rich and brilliant literature, — that of the Langue d'Oc.

The name of Romance has been applied

to those languages which were spoken in Italy, Gaul, and Spain, and which were formed from a mixture of the common speech of Roman colonists and soldiers with the language of conquered Gauls and conquering Germans. Distinct from the classic Latin of the Schools, the Law, and the Church, they were despised as bad Latin for a long time, but gradually formed themselves into groups, which we recognize to-day as Italian, French, Provençal, Spanish, etc.

The Provençal or Langue d'Oc was spoken in Guienne and Poitou, Toulouse and Provence: the first three principalities acknowledged the suzerainty of the French king, although their allegiance sat but lightly upon them; the latter was a portion of the Holy Roman Empire. One very marked characteristic of their civilization was the power and civil freedom of their great cities, whose institutions dated from the period of Roman occupation, and which were centres of wealth, learning, and refinement. Their exquisite language had here become highly developed and polished by their poets, who sang in melodious strains of love and war, of the spring-tide with its flowers and birds, the running streams that sparkled in the sunshine, the blue sky that bent so tenderly above them.

The Troubadours, as their poets were called, from the word *troubar*, to invent, were for the most part gay gentlemen and gallant warriors, who, like William of Acquitaine and Richard the Lion-Heart, were equally skillful with lance and lute, or stately dames, like Eleanor of Guienne and Eleanor of Provence, who practiced the art upon which they smiled.

Moreover, the Troubadours were ardent in devotion to some ladye-fair, in honor of whom they were always ready to indulge, not only in high-flown praise, but in extraordinary and fantastic adventures, worthy of Don Quixote himself, although they were far less constant in affairs of the heart than that chivalrous hero.

The Jongleurs, or professional minstrels,

were often attached to the personal service of a great baron or lady, and sang the songs of the Troubadours more commonly than their own, while they frequently added to their musical attainments great proficiency in sleight-of-hand performances. They also sometimes became strolling glee-men, wandering from place to place, and present on fair and market-days, accompanied, it might be, by an ape, who was trained to the performance of amusing tricks.

Life was rich and charming in Southern Gaul; democratic institutions flourished in her cities, her fertile soil,

" Where new pollen on the lily-petal grows
And still more labyrinthine buds the rose,"

gave abundantly of its fruits, and man, nature, and art rejoiced together.

But freedom of thought grew up in this free atmosphere; the famous heresy of the Albigenses, so called from the city of Alby, in the county of Toulouse, spread over the country, and was supported by Count Raymond himself, while it provoked the wrath of the Pope Innocent III., who found in the zeal of Montfort and the cupidity of Philip Augustus implements ready to his hand, and the thirty-years horror of the Albigensian war trampled out the fair civilization of Toulouse in fire and blood.

But the Langue d'Oc not only obtained in those lands where it was the speech of the people; its literary precedence made it the court language of the kings of Aragon and Navarre, whose sway extended at that time north of the Pyrenees, and also of the princely courts of northern Italy, whose poets neglected the yet rude dialects of their own land in favor of their more polished sister.

About this time, also, is the period of the Trouvères, the poets of the old French, or Langue d'Oil, who give us the *chansons de gestes*, among which stands first the noble "Song of Roland;" while Germany, like the England of Elizabeth, was "a nest of singing birds." The Minnesaenger were the contemporaries of the Troubadours and the Trouvères, and Barbarossa and his son Henry wrote verses in German and Provençal, as well as governed empires, and led armies into battle.

The first poets, in any Italian dialect, whose works remain, were the poets of Sicily, who, at the court of their all-accomplished master, King Frederick, essayed to sing in native strains. It was but a short-lived poetry, however, perishing when the promise of its lovely birth-place was destroyed, as that of Toulouse had been, by the united forces of the papacy and the French, and it was reserved for the Tuscan to become, through the genius of Dante, the mistress of the dialects of Italy.

THE GUELFS AND THE GHIBELLINES.

At the beginning of the reign of Conrad III. the first Hohenstaufen Emperor, the imperial crown was contested by Henry the Proud, Duke of Saxony. In a battle between the opposing parties the Saxons used as their war-cry the name of their leader, Duke Henry's brother, Welf, while the Swabian army responded with shouts of "Waibling!" a name derived from that of the village where their leader, Conrad's brother, had been born.

The names, transplanted into Italy, became Guelf and Ghibelline, and long survived as the titles of two hostile political parties, that of the Popes and that of the Emperors.

DANTE'S IMPERIALISM.

Dante's ardent imperialism is well known to all who have read the story of "the banished Ghibelline;" but it is quite possible that all may not understand in precisely what that imperialism consisted.

He accepted absolutely the mediæval theory of the two divinely-appointed heads of the world, the spiritual and the temporal, the Pope and the Emperor. He lived during the pontificate of Boniface VIII., who arrogated to himself temporal as well as spiritual supremacy, showing himself to the multitudes who thronged the streets of Rome during the Great Jubilee of the year 1300, seated upon a throne, and holding in his hands two swords, while he cried with a loud voice, "I am Cæsar!"

In the year 1312 that wise and powerful sovereign, Henry of Luxemburg, came to Rome, where he received the golden crown of the empire. He died soon after, unhappily, and with him perished all the hopes of the Ghibellines, but he was the ideal ruler to whom the Florentine patriot looked for the regeneration of the world.

Dante's doctrinal orthodoxy is testified to by the fact that, although he praises Frederick II. for good laws and wise government, he has plunged him, for free-thinking, into the flames of hell; but he greatly reprobated the Popes' assumption of temporal sway, which he believed contrary to their duty as spiritual chiefs.

To Dante, moreover, who had witnessed

the horrors of perpetual civil warfare, who had eaten the bitter bread of exile and toilsomely climbed "the stairs of others," it seemed, not unnaturally, that the one earthly good most to be desired is *peace*. This blessing he held to be attainable only under the sway of a monarch, the divinely appointed Emperor, who was placed so far above the strifes and jealousies of parties that he could deal impartial justice, and preserve peace and orderly rule for mankind.

But this monarch, all-powerful though he be, "is," says Dean Milman, "no arbitrary despot, but a constitutional sovereign; he is the Roman Law impersonated in the Emperor; a monarch who should leave all the nations, all the free Italian cities, in possession of their rights and old municipal institutions."

CHIEF PERSONS OF THE POEM.

GHIBELLINES.

Frederick II. of Hohenstaufen, fourth King and Emperor of the Swabian House; King of Germany, Burgundy, Lombardy, Sicily, and Jerusalem, Emperor of the Romans.

Ecelin of Romano, called the Monk; a great Ghibelline baron of Northern Italy, the most powerful noble in the Trevisan March. He rose to power under previous emperors, and was much favored by Frederick, but was now desirous of retiring from the world. He was one of the *Paterini* (the sufferers, or the resigned), a sect akin to the Albigenses of southern Gaul, to the Italian *Cathari* and the Armenian Paulicians. They included in their number not only many of the townsfolk, but of the barons of Lombardy. Like their Northern brethren they were proceeded against with great cruelty by the Popes. A crusade was inaugurated against them under the lead of the Preaching Friars, and many hundreds were put to death. Ecelin's first wife, represented in the poem as the mother of Palma, was Agnes, the sister of Azzo of Este; his last was Adelaide, a Tuscan lady; she was the mother of his two sons, Ecelin III., called the Tyrant, and Alberic, who succeeded to their father's lands and power in Lombardy. They were both cruel and oppressive in their rule, and both were finally slain by their wretched subjects.

Taurello Salinguerra, a great warrior and a skillful politician, with all the accomplishments of his day. He is devoted to the service of his over-lord Ecelin of Romano, in whose interests he is completely absorbed. He married for his first wife Retrude, of the family of the Hohenstaufen, who perished at Vicenza in a midnight insurrection; her son was supposed to have perished with her, but was saved, and is the Sordello of our story. He is hidden by Adelaide, who by her magic arts sees in Taurello those signs of greatness which show him destined to accomplish much if he have an end to work for. She hopes by depriving Taurello of his child to secure his entire service for her husband. Salinguerra's subsequent history is told us in the poem.

Palma, otherwise Cunizza, is the daughter of Ecelin the Monk. She became the wife of St. Boniface, and the heroine of many adventures. Legend says that she fell in love with Sordello, for whom she deserted her husband; she was afterwards twice married. Dante places her in Paradise, in the Heaven of Venus. She is represented in the poem as desiring to marry Sordello, whom she would inspire with her own Ghibelline sentiments, and raise to a prominent post under the Emperor.

Adelaide, wife of Ecelin the Monk. She is said to have practiced magic arts, to foresee the future, to learn what was going on at a distance, and to restore her own failing strength.

Tito, a Tyrolese, envoy of the Emperor to Taurello Salinguerra.

GUELFS.

Honorius III., Pope. He died in 1227. He was a man of great ability, and bent upon enforcing the theory of the papal supremacy. He sanctioned the establishment of the Dominican and Franciscan Friars. The quarrel with Frederick in regard to the Crusade began in his reign, but it did not come to extremities until the pontificate of his successor, Gregory IX.

Azzo, Marquis of Este, } Lombard
Count Richard of St. Boniface, } barons.

The Papal Legate.

Sordello. The Sordello of the poem is represented as the supposed son of an archer, El Corte by name, who has been brought up by Adelaide, wife of Ecelin of Romano, at her castle of Goito. His father had saved the life of Adelaide and her son in the same midnight fray in which the wife and child of Salinguerra were said to have perished, and as he had been killed in the fight his son has been cared for out of gratitude for the father's service. The youth becomes at last the favored minstrel of Romano's daughter, Palma, who gives him her love, and having learned his true parentage from the dying Adelaide, proclaims Sordello to be, not the archer's child, but the son of Taurello Salinguerra.

As for the Sordello of history the stories are many and various that are told of him, some writers thinking that there were two persons of the same name, whose deeds have been confounded, — the one the Troubadour, the other, an able and just Podestà[1] of Mantua. One writer would have us believe that the latter, who is said to have been a Ghibelline, is the Sordello whom Dante and Virgil meet in Purgatory, and to whom Benvenuto da Imola alluded as *nobilis et prudens miles et curialis*.

Raynouard, in his "Poetry of the Trou-

---

[1] Head of the city government; generally appointed by the Emperor.

badours," declares him to have been a Mantuan, the son of a poor knight, named El Corte; he says, that being fond of verse-making, Sordello came to the court of Count Richard of St. Boniface at Mantua, where he was much honored. Here, "for the sake of pastime," he made love to the Count's wife, Cunizza, and finally ran away with the lady, being urged thereto by her brothers, who had quarreled with Richard. He afterwards came to the court of Raymond Berenger, Count of Provence, who, like his wife, was a great friend of poets, and here he won, not only great renown, but a fine castle and a gentlewoman for his wife.

The Mantuan Chroniclers assert that he was of the Visconti family, that he married the daughter of Romano, and governed well and wisely as the Emperor's Podestà and Vicar-General of Northern Italy.

A Troubadour, according to yet another writer, who wrote much in the Provençal language, not of love, but of philosophy.

Although this statement seems hardly borne out by the poems that remain, it may have reference to some of those of which "Naddo" speaks with such disapproval. One of his most famous productions is a funeral song for Blancasso, a distinguished knight and troubadour.

According to still another biographer he was born at Goito, a village near Mantua, being the son of a poor knight, El Corte, and became St. Boniface's minstrel, falling in love with his wife and taking refuge in Provence, where he came to great advancement; returning thence he was made governor of Mantua, and died full of years and honors.

He is reported to have received the prize of bravery in a tourney from St. Lewis of France.

He wrote not only in the fashionable Provençal, but also in his native Italian, although none of his poems in the latter language remain.

For this Dante, in his treatise *De Volgari*

Eloquio, bestows upon him great praise. He says that there was at that time a city-speech, which was understood by all cultivated people in all parts of Italy, and commends Sordello that he made use of this rather than of a country dialect, which must be comprehensible to but few. This, also, is the reason why Browning speaks of him as the precursor of Dante.

It has been said that like most of the Troubadours, Sordello was a Ghibelline; in that case he would hardly have been attached to the household of St. Boniface, or on such terms with that bitter foe of the Hohenstaufen, the cruel Charles of Anjou, as to have been invited by the latter to accompany him on a crusade. The minstrel's answer reminds us of the passage in Browning's poem, in which our hero wishes for "firmer arm and fleeter foot, but no mad wings."

"My Lord Count," he says, "you ought not thus to ask one to face death. Every one is seeking his salvation by sea; but for my own part I am not eager to obtain it. My wish is to be transported to another life as late as possible." In fact it would seem as if Sordello must have gradually risen to a place among the Troubadours, who were for the most part gentlemen of rank; his original position in the household of St. Boniface being, perhaps, more clearly indicated by the term Jongleur. Still we do find Jongleurs who were knights as well; for example the famous Taillefer, the favorite minstrel of William of Normandy, who rode in front of the invading army at the battle of Senlac, tossing his sword into the air, and catching it as it fell, while he sang gayly the "Song of Roland."

In a long *teuson*, or poetical debate, between Sordello and a brother Troubadour, we find the question under discussion to be, which is preferable, love or glory, and the Mantuan pronounces without qualification in favor of the former.

Still another tradition seems to point to him as a son of Salinguerra, and this Browning has adopted, and from the many varying characteristics has shaped his hero, whom we must accept as the poet has given him to us, holding him, for the time at least, to be the Sordello, not only of the poem, but of history as well.

Unless we do this we shall miss the whole force of the comparison and contrast with Dante, and so one of the most striking features of the poem.

THE STORY OF THE POEM.

Say not the struggle naught availeth,
   The labor and the wounds are vain,
The enemy faints not, nor faileth,
   And as things have been, they remain.

If hopes were dupes, fears may be liars,
   It may be, in the smoke concealed;
Your comrades chase even now the fliers,
   And, but for you, possess the field.

ARTHUR HUGH CLOUGH.

THE STORY OF THE POEM.

BOOK I.

"WHO will," says Browning, "may hear Sordello's story told." As from the mountain-top Don Quixote beheld, amid the dust and din of multitudes, the great king, Pentapolin of the Iron Arm, struggling bravely in the press, so the poet has singled out a fellow-singer, seen dimly through the gloom of "six long sad hundred years," and presents him to us.

The poem opens in Verona, a city of Lombardy, in the early part of the thirteenth century, when Frederick II. is Emperor, and Honorius III.[1] is Pope. The old

[1] If Sordello, "born with the new century," is thirty years old when the story opens, it might seem that the Pope should be Gregory IX. Honorius died in 1227; an interregnum of two years followed, when Gregory was chosen.

strife of the Guelfs and Ghibellines is going on as usual; Count Richard of St. Boniface, the Lord of Mantua, has allied himself with Azzo, Marquis of Este, to overturn the power of Taurello Salinguerra, the right hand of Ecelin of Romano, who is the most powerful Ghibelline baron of Northern Italy and much trusted by the Emperor.

The news has just reached Verona that, caught in their own toils, the Guelfic chiefs have been taken captive at Ferrara, and the citizens are gathered together in the marketplace, eagerly discussing the event.

"Ah," says one, "Taurello's power did certainly seem to be on the wane; Ecelin has withdrawn into a monastery, where he is slowly dying of a wasting sickness; the Cæsar delays his coming, looked for long since, and the papal party has been gaining strength. The Guelfs in Ferrara rebuilt their ruined houses, believing themselves secure; it has even been asserted that two chiefs of the rival parties, meeting in a narrow street, crowded full of Ghibellines, actually passed without a fight. Such a state of things is too unnatural to last. Then Taurello, assuming his presence to be the sole obstacle to a permanent peace, left Ferrara for Padua. But no sooner was he gone than there was a Guelfic rising, rioting began, — lo! in an instant Taurello was in their midst and took a signal vengeance. Azzo fled, and, returning with St. Boniface, laid siege to the city; at length a parley was called, and the two Guelfs entered the town, over whose deserted streets rested an ominous silence; suddenly they were seized with all their train, and thrown into prison, and Salinguerra triumphed."

Such are the tidings that have reached Verona, and all are agog for battle!

The Emperor, delaying for the moment his projected crusade, proposes to come to Lombardy; he is very unwilling that the Pope should succeed in regaining any of the privileges which have been won in the past by Otto the Great and Barbarossa, and so defers his Syrian expedition until matters are more settled at home; an act for which he is excommunicated by Honorius. "Ecelin's father," say the Veronese, "was Ecelo, who came into power under Conrad III., receiving large fiefs in Northern Italy, which he has transmitted to his son, the present lord, who received additional favors from Frederick I. Ecelin is Lord of Romano, high in imperial favor, and the father of many sons and daughters, and, despite his hard heart and sickly person, has thriven greatly in the world, which he has now so inexplicably resolved to abandon. His prime support is Salinguerra, a superb, easy-going chieftain, whose life has, however, been a lonely one. Years ago wife and child perished in a party fray, and careless of himself, he has bent all his energies to prop the House of Romano." "Are these," ask the Veronese burghers, "the leaders to compare with Azzo of Este, the Guelfic Lion?"

All night long the people talk and listen; all night long the Twenty-Four, the magistrates of Verona, sit in solemn debate together; and in a small inner chamber of the palace are Palma, the daughter of Romano, and Sordello, the hero of our tale, the precursor of Dante, as a singer in the native tongue of Italy. Who is Sordello, and why is he here in the secret room, with the great baron's daughter? This is the story which the poet proceeds to tell us.

About the city of Mantua the land is half slough half pine forest, with water-courses fringed with scarlet-oaks and maples; in summer even the Mincio is dry; but in winter it is one broad morass, but half redeemed by human toil to human uses. Some thirty years before the scene we have described, the castle of Goito stood almost alone in such a recovered spot, surrounded by low mountains, whose main defiles were hidden by firs and birches and bound about with vineyards.

A castle full of winding corridors and noble rooms, one of which, maple-paneled, and ornamented with Arabic inscriptions in burnished gold, was hung with arras, on which were pictured the proud barons and fair dames of the House of Romano, while yet beyond, in a vaulted chamber, stood a font of stone, encircled by a group of marble maidens, by whom, for many a year, Sordello was wont to sit at eventide, and pray that they might win pardon for the sins for which he fancied them to be doing penance in stone.

Sordello is a slender boy, in page's dress, who watches the birds in the autumn days, and spends his hours in winter in gazing at the forms depicted on the arras.

He is a princely boy, whom nature seems to have formed for pleasure, — one of the regal class, separated from the mass of men who are doomed to toil, and placed among that smaller company whose birthright is to enjoy. As some lands, like his own Italy, are framed for rich fertility, lands where all nature rejoices in production.

They absorb at eye and ear the loveliness of nature, while to those less favored she holds her beauty but half revealed, as if she could not trust them with her world.

How can this regal class love? Like souls brooding upon each richly-laden discovery, blind at first to anything beyond its beauty, until such great love becomes oppressive, and could they realize, as sometimes befalls such natures, how little they can do of good, how little they can bring of blessing to the object which they worship, their love would become to them not a blessing, but a curse. Hence it is given them to be capable of investing lifeless things with life from their own souls, while one by one their idols are discrowned as they are able to behold things more and more beautiful, until they gaze upon the Highest. One characteristic is always theirs, the need to blend themselves with external things, and to belong to what they worship, until that which they adore holds them forever in its grasp, past hope of escape. They lay aside their individuality, and abdicate their throne; the creator yields to the creature;

they give life to others, but they lose their own.

There is another class of natures that, looking at beauty no less eagerly, refer each form of outward loveliness to some related loveliness within their own souls, believing it but the outward manifestation of an inner consciousness, the physical realization of an intellectual dream.

The homage that others direct outward they turn inward, and wonder that external circumstances can depress the soul, which can laugh at fate, and, stamped with individuality and unfettered by the elemental life of earth, can soar to Heaven's complexest essence, equal to being all.

Can this indeed be true, and is our race really vindicated by the ascent of these lofty souls whom we, one day, may follow even with our more bounded wills?

But how sad it is to find that minds of the first order may be enervated by certain moods that counsel them to slumber and inaction, instead of bidding them stoop to task themselves for the good of mankind when life and time are in accord for action, because, forsooth, the occasion is not suited to display all their powers. "Why do so small a deed? Wait till the grand adventure offer!"

And there is something yet worse that may happen, for the soul may be filled with a desire to put forth all its powers at once, to reach beyond mortal limits, and to force into time the work of eternity; to be Cæsar or nothing; to refuse a part if the whole be not placed within its grasp.[1]

Such is Sordello; but who sees the plague-spot on him as he loiters here?

Born with the new century, in the midst of the glow and flowering beauty that are spreading from the barbarism of the past, as witnessed to by a stray Greek, now and then wandering through Florence, the pre-

---

[1] The effort to realize the impossible, the search for new excitement, became incessant, till thought and caprice, judgment and fantasy, became indistinguishable.— "King Louis of Bavaria," *London Spectator*.

cursor of a glory that a later age shall bring; fortunate should be Sordello, and who sees now the plague-spot? And yet it is there, and though for a while we may cover it from view, it shall some day work woe to one for whom there is yet much of pleasantness in his daily life.

He can never remember when he has not dwelt at Goito, that castle set in the marshland, which belongs to Adelaide, Ecelin's Tuscan wife. He has known no other world, but this has been his own, to wander through and loiter in at will, so he do not enter the northern rooms, where Adelaide's apartments are. Here he is attended by foreign serving-women, who have been kind to the lonely boy.

And for a time the day's life was enough for Sordello, who sucked the sweets of earthly pleasures and wreathed each new discovery with childish fantasies, seeking to put something of his own rich life into lifeless things, that they might become in some sense his fellows. They appear with aspects never quite the same, depicted as his fancy wills, which sometimes bestows upon familiar things grotesque shapes, though keeping a grave regard through all. Each was related to each; the house-leek on the roof had some bond that allied it with the proud chieftain, who came one day with his archer-train to the lodge, and strode clanking up the stair to those chambers that were closed to Sordello.

Like a spider he spun the web of his fancies over all, and swung gayly upon the threads that were produced from his own fertile imagination. And if he were selfish in his pleasures, who had ever taught him that others might gladly share his joy? And when chance destroyed his pretty fancies, as must needs happen since the world is always ready to sweep away such webs; if the March winds beat down a heron's nest, or a fawn fell from a crag to die, could such things break the charm that held the boy enthralled?

Time brought at last to Sordello what the

world should have taught him, namely, the true relationship between himself and his companions, whom, although the glamour has departed, he cannot yet wholly renounce, since they have once afforded him delight. If, however, he now try to recall the poppy's gifts, he sees that it is but a poppy after all; no longer some enchanted creature, which felt with him, as he with it. Why should he distrust the evidence of sense? 'Tis but a poppy. Then speaks the new-born judgment, declaring it to be of little use to discern the attributes of others, if destitute of attributes one's self. Or even if it were of use, if one could only possess some special office that was one's very own! Or if not that, at least his soul craved some justification for the wish to circumscribe and concentrate, rather than increase, the sum of actual pleasure, and prove, beyond a doubt, that mere sympathy suffices, and that one can enjoy delights by proxy.

Alas for Sordello, if he reason thus! For from the beginning love is whole and true, and is sure of its own truth, if of nothing else; it will not endure to have its face gazed upon by a crowd that cannot know the deep pulses of its heart. Its very inability to minister worthily to what it worships only increases its strength of feeling, and exalts the idol it adores far above itself, and exalts it gladly. But souls like Sordello's, if they are coerced and shamed, yet still retain their power of will, care but little, and comfort themselves in some mysterious fashion, although they are constantly peering forth to see if others approve of their claims, and will utter for them the thoughts they cannot themselves express. Such minds as this must always be in the presence of a crowd.

"Vanity," says Naddo, who is the personification of general common-sense and average public opinion.

But how shall the lonely Sordello find a public? Forth comes, not only every painted warrior from the arras, every stone girl from the fountain, not only Adelaide, whom once, being astray in the castle, he had surprised, as she sat reading, a fair maiden at her knee; not only these, but the whole outside world as he had imaged it from song and story and, perhaps, from dreams; its characteristics, such as he had fancied them and transferred them to tree and flower, not thinking any of them sufficient to bestow upon a man, — these now stood forth independent and alone. Strength, wisdom, grace disengaged themselves, and he began dimly to conceive of a sort of human life, or at least his brain teemed with life-like figures. But on what shall his attention be fixed? Are these figures merely to testify to the movements of Sordello's soul, terrible or sweet? Each one lives his own life, boasts of his own share of happiness, and stands alone somewhere, where his desires are easiest attained. But these are no longer desires which are easy to be realized, as were those of his forest-creatures; contrasts and combinations are presented by this company so suddenly evoked, — combinations which are prized by them who are, perhaps, to become judges of his own desires. Shall he suffer this crowd of his own creations to win control, to arbitrarily give value to what he has lived without, and never felt the lack of? What matters it? A deeper power has rendered Sordello discontented with the woodland sights which lately so enwrapped him, and he is absorbed in studying the characters and purposes of the human fancies which he has called into being, and whose artificial joys he accepts, not as he views them, but that, employing each shape to estimate the value of the others, he may be enabled to enter into a multitude of authorized pleasures, as once he blent himself with tree and flower, and even more completely, surely, than with them. Each of these creatures, who is, in a fashion, Sordello himself, is capable of great deeds; one day he will accomplish such, though now he must dwell with dreams; yet by their aid he will find self-expression, an instrument serviceable in the future. Why should he not be the peer of Ecelin, who, he hears, is become the Emperor's viceroy? Surely he can wield a brand as well. He makes the trial, but failing, returns to those easier dreams of future triumphs, which fancy can portray at will.

Thus he lives, no longer free from care, but comforted for his deprivations, fitting himself by anticipation to play his part nobly in the future, when great barons shall do him reverence, and great cities witness his triumph.

Who grudges time spent for such ends? Rather labor to concentrate qualities, selected from far and near, and testing them, compress the finest into one perfection, and grasp the whole at once.

And thus he treated his phantasms; setting aside the simpler, and combining traits, he formed one or two characters that took up into themselves the virtues of humanity, and these in turn were reduced to one all-powerful and all-noble. Whose is this transcendent figure? Can it be Frederick,

of whom the bowmen talked? Is the juice
which he knows is bubbling in the stalk of
yonder grape-vine some Saracenic wine
which the Cæsar is drinking with the Miramoline?[1] Are those hazel nuts, perchance,
the dates upon the bough that John of
Brienne sent to hasten the sailing of the
crusading squadron, as of old Cato held up
the ripe figs in the Roman Senate House to
show how near Rome's rival, Carthage, lay?
Is it in truth the Cæsar? But how difficult
for harsh sights and sounds to come from
the sad world to one who must dwell in perfect serenity, since his least look or word is
mighty to control, and his right hand wields
the thunderbolt! But thunder would be
needless if the multitude would but listen to
the song of the minstrel; why should not
this all-perfect being be the Poet? And so,
half emperor, half minstrel, he lived his life;
only vile things troubled him, and these in

---

[1] A Moslem prince, whose territory was situated in Northern Africa. Miramoline is another form of the hame, which is a Spanish corruption of a Moorish title.

thought he slew; while other fancies he controlled, and others yet he placed in seats of honor, enthroned a little lower than himself.

Like many before and after him, Sordello had found Apollo! He would be a poet, although as yet he was forced to steal from others, and to appear in a poetic array that was but a sad patchwork. In the rare June days he climbed the ravines, where the sparkling runnels slipped over clattering pebbles, through the green walls of lindens roofed with vines, whence emerging, he beheld long lines of trees which closed into a magic forest, still, as of old, full of sweet surprises.

Gradually he sees the Pythons perish before him; obstacles are overcome; but the maids, his Delian priestesses, linger still; more or less loving or disdainful, they join in adoring Apollo. But where is the Daphne, the beloved of the God?

He hears the serving-women gossip of the probable marriage of Ecelin's daughter,

Palma, with Richard of St. Boniface, the Guelfic prince, that thus political feuds may be appeased. "But," they add, "Palma will have none of him!"

And so the lady who scorns other mates seems most worthy of Sordello, and becomes the Daphne of his dreams.

Time wears on, though Fate delays to provide the stage and the audience Sordello desires. He grows pale and restless in his enforced quiet, weary of inaction. Time flies, but he remains the same. None come to him. Adelaide is in Mantua, whence Taurello has departed. Oh, let but Frederick come, and let matter be found for that minstrelsy which has been lured from Sicily and the young Emperor's court, and which, like the double outflow of a drinking-cup, sparkles over the thirsty land, to Provence on the north and thus far to the south!

Ah, what a way this is to tell men of what is going on about them, recording it in the very tongue which they speak daily, as the Troubadours do, while in their turn the

Trouvères proclaim the wonder, and explain it to their hearers, until the House of Romano is famed throughout the world! Such was Taurello's purpose when he introduced the poetic games, the Courts of Love and Song, into Lombardy; and Adelaide, in her turn, now summons one at Mantua, when a sudden accident, like a flash of light, opens Sordello's eyes to the true work of life.

BOOK II.

IT is a pleasant spring morning, and Sordello is sure that the day will bring him to the lady of his dreams. She is there in the whispering pine woods, and he has but to seek her. Gayly he sets forth; the great morass sparkles wide around him in the sunshine, and Palma's form floats vaguely before his eyes; the marshy ground yields beneath his tread, lakes spreading as he moves; Palma enters the wood; she will emerge on the other side, and crowds, and St. Boniface also, will see that she loves him. One more screen of pines is passed, and lo! Mantua lies before him, and upon the green plain without the walls cluster real men and women about a gorgeous pavilion. But do they all rush to adore Sordello? Not so; and yet his fancies were not wholly vain, for there sits

Palma, seen in the pavilion as the curtains fall aside. Now he believes that his hour had come; — yet not so; — for Eglamor, the best minstrel of St. Boniface, steps forward to conclude with his song the Court of Love. He sings the praise of Elys, the lady of his love, in whose honor they name the new string just fastened to his lute, and all the hearers burst forth into applause. But spite of the beauty of the song, Sordello believes himself capable of surpassing it, of giving it a more fitting ending; and scarcely have the shouts died away when he seizes a lute, and filling up the outline Eglamor had drawn, makes it living with the glow of his own ardent imagination. On flies the song, barely able to keep pace with the rushing action, until Naddo is aghast. He is like some Egyptian, who, goading a bull with his sharp prong, suddenly sees him turn his head, and beholds beneath his tongue the scarabæus, the mystic sign that marks the sacred apis. The people shout for joy; Sordello shrinks, but is sustained by the sight of Adelaide, at her side the maid of the north chamber, the Palma and Daphne of his dreams. How fair she is with her blue eyes and locks of gold! and as she unwinds a scarf from her neck, and lays it upon his shoulders, Sordello's senses fail, and he knows no more, until he awakens in his old home, his forehead crowned, and Palma's gift about him, while on the floor beside him lies a splendid vesture, the prize of victory. The kindly serving-women gather around him, and praise him for a youth so spent as to fit him for such deeds, and they tell him how Eglamor, overwhelmed by defeat, has died, and that he has been chosen to be Palma's minstrel, and has been brought home by the Jongleurs in a body.

Sordello, who hitherto had only perceived, now rose up to think; he passed a week in living over again in memory all the delightful event. What wonderful thing had he then done? Blind was the other not to see, as quickly as he had done, the relative importance of each part. But would he, Sordello, have ever turned from Elys, to sing of her for the pleasure of song itself? True, the bits of verse did help him to find a new beauty in himself, leading his thought up to many a hoard of fancies. Why should such a performance win applause from men if they, too, had fancies? Was it possible that they found a beauty in the song itself? "If," he thinks, "they can find in the poem any such beauty as I can, who in my fancy have lived what then I sang, who, in my dreams, have enjoyed what now I praise; if they can do that, they must hold me, who could make them do it, for a very god indeed! Or it may be that some one like Eglamor, who, if beneath me, is above them, may have set a stamp upon our work, so that men believe and worship what they neither truly know nor delight in. They may, too, have fancies of their own, which will not come at their beck, but are undefined until song links them together, and renders them distinct and palpable."

Suddenly the wind is hushed, the noon-day sky is clouded, and Sordello hears the tramp of footsteps through the pine wood, as the minstrel company bear the body of Eglamor to his last resting-place, calm in death, a few flowers in his hand. He was Sordello's opposite; for him verse was a temple-worship, a ceremony that unveiled the sanctuary, nor did he ever repine at the effort needed to stand therein, or at finding much that was blank and uncertain at the shrine before which he was wont to kneel, until the power responded, vouchsafing him some sight or sound which he made his own, and fixed, beautiful forever, in poetic form. And these were a part of his life, unloosed at pleasure, to soothe pain or care, while he faltered like Perseus when he set free Andromeda, so far these fancies seemed beyond himself. Yet he was no rare genius, transfiguring in every element at will, but rather some patient gnome, who, shut up in some cavern with his agate cup, his seed-pearl and his topaz rod, finds enough to do in making the best disposal that he can of them.

And he had loved his art, and possessing little of the world's wealth, had cared not for the world's coldness, since he had that sweet gift that makes all others poor, — the gift of song. None yet had equaled him, and the coming triumph had seemed to him so certain, his lay so fervid, unsurpassed as yet.

We know the sequel, how he lost the victory, and rank and life. Yet envy had sunken within him when he had listened to Sordello, and he tried to shout like the others, though not like the common sort, to show his pleasure, and, bending down, he placed his own crown beneath Sordello's, and kissed his successor's hand, leaving a tear upon it. And then he joined his band, who bade him sing his rival's song; he obeyed them, and went home. There was no crowd, as of yore, to welcome him at his coming; all were gone to escort the new minstrel, his rival. And so he lay down to sleep, well knowing that in the morning he must rise to confront the problem of his changed estate; and death, less cruel than his friends, took him before the dawning.

Then the minstrels, who had heard of Sordello's romantic home, and believed, with Naddo, that one would willingly rest far from the scene of one's defeat, had borne the dead poet to Goito, and Sordello, rising a degree higher yet in soul, laid his own crown upon the breast of the dead, and committed the charge of the minstrel's dust and of his fame to the ferns and pines. Nor was his prayer fruitless; for a trefoil floweret, that whitens ere noontide and is swept away by the breeze of evening, bears still the name of Eglamor.

It was a month of May, and Sordello, robed and filleted, lay with his lute upon the flowery turf; spite of the glow of his poet-life, something within him seemed to whisper that this fortune could not endure. He had sought to learn something of his birth and station, and he had been told this. Years before, Ecelin, engaged in a feud at Vicenza, had fired the quarter of the town in which his enemies dwelt, although that very night his son Ecelin had been born there. The latter, with his mother, was with difficulty rescued by Elcorte, an archer. The wrath of those who missed the greater prey vented itself yet more fiercely upon that within their grasp, and it was said that among those who perished were the wife and only son of Taurello Salinguerra. Then the archer's deed seemed daring enough to merit large reward, and since he himself had fallen, his son had been carefully nurtured at Goito, to which place Adelaide had escaped. And this archer's son was Sordello! Apollo vanishes, and there remains a low-born youth, who has just been named his lady's minstrel. Is this he who, as our poet wildly fancies, is to be proclaimed the monarch of the world?

For Sordello, who had been a slave to longings, suppressed save in his dreams, not daring to claim his desired mastery until he had decked himself with strength, grace, and wisdom to fit him for his throne, has now resolved to claim his kingdom. He has determined, relying upon his will[1] alone, to do his best with what he has, and let the rest go by. The die is cast; never again can Sordello be to himself one of the many, nor feel that for him and for the many there is a common law, since Apollo's presence has exempted him from that. Men now are no more his equals than were bud and flower in the olden time; although inactive himself, he is greater than those who act, since each stoops to his star, to acquire from it his function; he has gained the same result with meaner mortals, who are trained to express their one ruling thought, since he is capable of comprehending all ideas, and can take power from Richard, or grace from Palma, and mix these qualities, or enjoy them separately, as best pleases him; so he is never cramped or restricted by

[1] In this, as in other places in the poem, Mr. Browning seems to use the word will, as equivalent to imagination, and the capacity to realize in himself all his images.

any specialty; never stamped strong, and so compelled to turn all his energies to strength, or wise, and forced to give evi-. dence of wisdom. Which means that there is no one Idea, which floats star-like above and before him, luring him on to its realization. "Fortunate," he cries, "that my flesh never strove to emulate so various a soul! Took no casual mould of the first fancy, and lay, clogged by it, averse to change; but has left her free to range, and, cast into the shade, hinders but little, if it cannot help! Let my soul range freely, expressing the quintessence of all beauty by being conscious of it itself; but surely the World, which can wonder at men who may themselves be filled with wonder, the World which loves at second-hand, and makes idols of those who bow in their turn before some idol, surely this World, when it shall behold me, must bow in unexampled worship!"

(Dear Monarch, notice how wide the breach here. Look down upon all men if you will, but why tell them your opinion of them?)

"Ah," thinks Sordello, "the world shall bow to me, who from afar see all the joys of man, or great or small, nor taste of them myself. I have no machine for exercising my will; mere consciousness be mine. Let them perceive what I could do, and believe in a mastery proven by my song, which shall show that all they are or would be, I am. I take no pains to change anything, vex them with no new forms, but give them just what they desire, that and no more; so that in me each shall behold and love that love which leads his own soul to perfection."

Thus Sordello chose, for his life's portion, <u>song, not deeds.</u> He put aside the emperor and remained the poet alone. Verse only for him! Strength should not seek to express itself in effort, nor grace in outward beauty, nor uttered wisdom control unseemly moods. It should be song alone. The blood and fire of the year, which so concern the world, are to him but a pastime, to wile away the hours until he shall step forth upon the stage.

And now that all is outlined, Sordello takes his ease, until there comes a letter from Naddo, who entreats him to return to Mantua to feed a famishing world. His fame has gone before him, and all bid him welcome, while all seem to Sordello angels, who are to be made supremely happy by his song.

Then he finds the task of singing an annoyance, since he had never cared for song itself, but only for its effect; of what use had song been in his past life, when all he had wished for had been praise, not the labor that earned the praise? His rhymes were Eglamor's; but Naddo upholds him before the people, and he determines to go on, remembering that if failure come he can betake himself once more to Goito.

We struggle with our glossaries to gain an idea of what the Troubadour would express in his varied poems, but we never quite comprehend what there was in them that so moved the people, as he drew out from the flood of the time its elements, and tracing actions backward to their source, added a touch or two, and made qualities men and women. Virtue and vice passed by in the persons of saint and sinner, and all the passions were incarnated by song. Praise was showered upon him, his fictions were held for realities, and he felt a desire to realize something of what he sang; to come down from his pedestal and accept the petty joys of actual life. By doing this, however, he would abjure the right to enjoy the quintessence of all, and thus would frustrate his main design; even for very love of it he must abjure all pleasure. He laughed; what sage but perishes if he look up from the pages of his magic book, because at the very first line he finds that his art has efficiency?

For a while our poet left his imaginings to try the stuff that held his images, his Language. No need to tell how he wrought upon that language, until from the rough speech of the men about him he had hammered out at last a rude armor, that should one day be more prized than the Roman panoply that had been melted to make it. And when it was complete he strove to use it. Took up an action with its actors, lived in each of his creatures, whom he equipped in the harness he had so toilsomely wrought. And then he bade the Mantuans listen. Vain attempt! The armor broke away piece by piece, because perceptions, such as he sought to clothe with it, are unfit for a garb so intellectual as language. Thought may replace perception, but can hardly coexist with it, since it is but the latter's presentment; offering us the whole in a series of parts, giving us by the successive and the many that which is really one and simultaneous. Does the crowd lack perception? It painfully tacks together the thoughts into which Sordello has torn perception, its office being to reconstruct, as his is to diffuse.

Hopeless of success, he returns to the old measures and sings the exploits of Montfort over the Albigensians. Even now he is not understood. His audience never guess that he depicts himself in his hero, and wonder how he comes to know so much about Montfort. What, after all, does he care for the Mantuans? But was he not in a way forced to help them, to treat them as if they were peers of the images of the old Goito days? He strewed fairy gold upon the multitude, but all in vain. The years went by, and Sordello disappeared from among men.

The man and the poet were hopelessly at war within him; the man refusing to be any longer fooled with fancies, while the poet would consecrate all his powers to song; and now one nature, now the other had its way. But the complete Sordello, man and poet, had gone forever. Now he resolved to put aside all but his art and compel the age to recognize a master; now to forswear song, fling by his lethargy, and play a man's part in life. Ere he could decide the Mantuans interfered. Why not settle down there among them? Remember that he was Palma's minstrel, and be glad to submit to established rules, nor fall into extravagant absurdities like Vidal [1] and others. But when he sought to answer their questions, his speech had the largeness of divine replies, too slow in condensing themselves to satisfy the citizens, with their little stock of opinions cut and dried, or questions youthfully crude. To answer questions asked would have been the work of a lifetime; he resorted to ready-made responses and often-repeated gestures. So his soul, unable to compass the whole, began to see less and less that was worth striving for in the parts. As man and poet alike he failed, and Naddo reproves him for not being able to sing a straightforward song, and persisting in trying to work out problems which, being no philosopher, he had better leave untouched. "For poetry," says Naddo,

[1] Pierre Vidal, a Troubadour, who followed Richard the Lion-Heart on the third crusade. He was even more renowned for his extravagant behavior than for his poetic gifts, and was involved in many remarkable adventures. Dante introduces him into the 26th Canto of the Purgatorio, putting into his mouth some verses of Provençal poetry.

"must be based on common sense. If you would have your songs endure, build upon the human heart, the general, healthy one." Many Naddos overwhelm him; he yields, strives to conform, and fails once more.

Meanwhile Adelaide has died, and Ecelin writes to Taurello that he shall never return to the world; that his two sons, Ecelin and Alberic, are to marry the niece of Azzo and the daughter of St. Boniface; that the Count himself is to have Palma, and thus peace will be made between the two contending factions. The news comes to Salinguerra at Naples, where he has lately joined Frederick, who is to sail within the month for Syria. Swiftly he rides to visit his lord, and remonstrate with him on his course; but to no purpose; these things, says Ecelin, must be as he has planned.

The country rings with the news of how Romano's great captain has withdrawn to Mantua, whither, although it is his native city, he never goes, unless dissatisfied with Ecelin. The city prepares great shows to greet him, and Sordello is chosen to bid him welcome; but no thoughts will come to him; he strolls out beyond the walls, and wanders aimlessly through the fields, until he finds himself unexpectedly at Goito, his old home, looking smaller than of yore, but more mysterious than ever. Palma, they tell him, has left that very day.

Once more Sordello lay beside the fountain, and his life passed in review before him. Body and Intellect both had failed; was it the fault of the Will? And he flung his crown into the fount, and laid aside the scarf that all so envied him. There was no poet the next day at Mantua, and Taurello, when the Masque was over, asked vainly for a song. None was forthcoming, and the good-natured soldier accepted a bull-baiting instead.

BOOK III.

ONCE more Goito has Sordello. The dream is over, and nature effaces the print of the past; the world's stain leaves our poet, and the Mantuans fade from his memory. Better is it, he feels, to be unrevealed than half revealed. Of what further use, then, is will? Why should he feel the need to become all natures, yet retain the law of his own? Will and the means of displaying it, he determines to abjure, save any that are so distinct that they may serve to amuse without tempting one to become anything. As he was at first, such will he now become.

A year passed with no great change in Sordello, save that the eyes once bright with questioning were now dulled by receiving. He slept, but he knew that he slept.

One dull, gray autumn day he sauntered

through the wood, his whole soul in harmony with the aspect of nature. His youth and nature's both were gone. And once gone, youth is gone forever; deeds passed by can never be achieved; nature may renew herself, but we —

"Alas!" sighs Sordello, "are all my chances forfeited? Have I not two lives that I may spend the one in learning how to live the other? Nature may retrieve her losses; my overthrow is final! No thoughts of love, meeting with Elys at the even-close; no hours of pleasure spent with Frederick and his court in gay carouse; no triumphant going like the blind Doge, Dandolo, through conquered Byzantium![1] No more of peace or war! Ah, these were the fragments of a whole, the rounds of a ladder, which I mistook for the broad platform it was meant to

---

[1] In 1204 the Latin Conquest of Constantinople took place. The leaders of the so-called crusade were the Doge of Venice, Dandolo, and Baldwin of Flanders, with others of less note. The first step was to conquer the city in behalf of an exiled prince, the next to seize upon it entirely and place Baldwin on the throne.

lift me to. Happiness did await me; life should be used to acquire; and such deeds conduced to teach me by a self-revelation, which was mistaken for the use itself. What helped to that was pleasure, what delayed was pain. I have laid down the ladder; I climb no more; but the platform stretches above me, and joys elude me of which till now I never had a glimpse. The multitude are endowed with some being, however slight, distinct from what they see, however limited; happiness must consist in feeding being by gleanings from things seen, in attaining the qualities of the latter, and thus becoming what one beholds. Such transmutation, the making what has been alien native to one's self, is the Use-of-Life. Ere I begin to truly exist I must include within myself a world I now know in spirit only, and then what would be left to me to blend with? But already my will is master of the world; yet it becomes thereby more alien to me, since my means are so unworthily suited to my will; I was bound to tread down forever these tantalizing joys. I die; but will the rest die also? Shall some future Sordello catch the clue I miss, which still seems at my hand, and still eludes my grasp? Have I wantonly abandoned the chance of solving the problem, and shall I, thrust aside, remain so, while beyond there passes a pageant that Time will never repeat? Nay, rather, slake my thirst at any spring!"

And with the thought comes Naddo to summon the poet to Verona. He tells him that Ecelin has parted his wealth between his two sons, Ecelin and Alberic, who are to wed Guelfic ladies, and abides still in his monastery; that Palma and St. Boniface are betrothed; how the Guelfs rose at Ferrara, and Salinguerra, having taken revenge, is now besieged there by Este and St. Boniface; and how the latter, once victory is gained, will marry Palma, absorb Romano, and inaugurate better government. Sordello is wanted by Palma, who doubtless wishes him to prepare a song for her wedding-feast. And now we have arrived at the point where our story opens. The news of the Guelfic discomfiture has reached Verona, and while the square is alive with excited burghers, Palma and her minstrel are sitting, as lovers, in the secret chamber. Palma strives to tell him her story. Sordello's had not been the only want that Goito had nurtured; Palma, destined to serve, as he to be served, had grown up there also. While Sordello had sought to lead nature captive, she had dreamed of some outsoul, for whose coming she pined, nor did she dare let heart and mind expand, until this mysterious power, for whom they grew, should appear to direct them. Everything in her life she felt must be determined by one who is to be to her the incarnation of a will, inscrutable save at one point, which would shine that her own powers might flow towards it. First whom to love, then how to love him. And hoping thus, from day to day she waited for his coming.

Then came the Love-Court, and one

face burst upon her, not seen for the first time. She dared not speak of her feelings, for, although Adelaide was silent, Palma felt certain that any schemes she might form would be frustrated by the wily Tuscan.

Then one night the Lady died, and none but Palma there, to whom the dying woman revealed many secrets of her life. Ecelin, arriving just as all was over, refused to carry out any of the wishes of his dead wife, since he cared no longer for family glory, and was only eager to return to his monastery. But Palma, alone at Goito, sought how to bring herself and Sordello together, and rejoiced to have Taurello teach her of the greatness of her house, and show her how Romano has become fixed in Italy. Other families have depended upon the Pope, Romano has relied upon the Emperor.

And as Adelaide [1] of Susa intrusted Pied-

---

[1] Adelaide of Susa, a great baroness of Lombardy, was a firm partisan of the Popes. Her daughter Bertha was the wife of the Emperor Henry IV., opponent of Hildebrand.

mont, which left to the Popes an open passage between France and Italy, to the great Countess Matilda[1] of Tuscany, so should Palma take into her charge the Trentine, which the Tuscan wife of Romano had desired to hold, as affording a safe way for Frederick between Germany and Italy, and there maintain her power by Salinguerra's help.

Taurello, meanwhile, had thought it expedient to temporize, and on the very day of the outrage at Ferrara he betrothed Palma to St. Boniface; and as the latter quitted Verona instantly for the siege, Palma came directly to the latter city, and being thus ready to confirm or annul the compact, put Richard in the wrong. And now, what glory may not come to Sordello through this

[1] Matilda, Countess of Tuscany, was a firm friend of Pope Gregory VII. It was at her castle of Canossa that the famous meeting between the Emperor Henry IV. and Pope Gregory took place. She bequeathed her dominions to the Holy See, and the question as to the feudal homage due for them was a source of many quarrels between the Popes and Emperors.

state of things? A month since Ecelin has taken monkish vows, but yet Salinguerra cannot definitely abandon his liege lord. He writes to ask if he shall still hold himself, as he is ready to be held, at his old master's orders, or if the sons of Romano are now the head of the House. The letter has been sent by Palma, and the answer is to be given by her. Her father refuses, once for all, to re-enter the world, and frees Taurello from all allegiance to himself. Lest Salinguerra be depressed by this, Palma has determined to take the place left vacant by her father and her brothers, and as the Kaiser's representative sanction the steps which Taurello wishes to take. She now urges Sordello to accompany her to Ferrara, whither she will go in minstrel's dress, and anticipating the various envoys, seek the presence of Salinguerra, whose brave words, she trusts, will teach her lover, what she believes the truth, — that the Emperor's cause is his own.

And so she leaves him. Ere the morning

dawns he has resolved that he will indeed be the gate-vein of Lombardy's heart's-blood, the soul of this body. Thus will he conquer fate though he be doomed to live apart, the core of this outer crust which he has vitalized.

And thus Sordello is brought to rejoice in the crowd's applause because one round of life has been achieved; he has found that a soul, however great, is insufficient to its own happiness, both in bodily organs and in the skill to manifest the imagination by means of them; and again to show to men that imagination, and oblige them to recognize that which is hidden by what has been revealed. He has learned also that, when the last struggle was over, the will which had been bidden to abdicate its throne and would not, might yet be allowed to reign, and would permit him to enjoy mankind. He sees now that it is his true duty to inspire the people to action, not merely to invite them to behold him acting the parts which should be theirs to play.

BOOK IV.

MEANTIME Ferrara is torn by the struggles of contending factions. Taurello has held a conference with the Emperor's envoy, whom he dismisses in apparent haste to make way for the deputies of the Eastern League, who are accompanied by the Papal Legate. The carrochs [1] of the various cities are drawn up in the square, which is filled with people and gay with flaunting banners. The citizens have striven to put as good a face as possible upon their disastrous condition, and they have crowded together to discuss affairs: some rejoice that Ecelin's banner is missing, but they are reminded that magic

---

[1] The carroch, or *carroccio*, was a huge wagon in which the standard of the city was carried into battle. It also bore a cross and a great bell. It was placed in the centre of the army, and zealously guarded from risk of capture.

arts may help him now, as they have done in his wife's lifetime, to a knowledge of what passes in his absence. We enter now a garden full of southern trees and blossoms, and adorned with statues, brought by Salinguerra from Messina to please his Sicilian bride, as was also the font at Goito, which he gave to Adelaide. But these statues are, like their owner, full of active life, able to right themselves. Here he holds Boniface imprisoned; here the envoys must come to sue for grace; and here we find Sordello, who has visited Este's camp and seen the envoys' march and the Papal train. Not now as when he held himself aloof, save for the fantastic tie he was willing to acknowledge; the more he regarded them, the less satisfied he now felt with the part he was playing. Was this the humanity he had raved over, and wished to become one with? Are all men notable alike? As well expect to find all Taurello's trees one pine. A pine does rise here and there, the rest are lowly shrubs. How few the chiefs of men! And yet the people grow, grow ever, until it seems as if each leader lost his individuality and became merely the head of absent Paduans or Tyrolese. While thus he meditated old memories returned with new effect, and before he was aware he and mankind were one; and yet the people seemed beneath him. What cared he for a mind here and there to repay him, if all the rest were base? Somehow he must establish an equilibrium, and secure for the many the long-possessed privileges of the few. He should think first of men and of their wants: when these were satisfied, then he should find room for the finer qualities of his own soul to act. He wondered now that when he had dreamed of ruling mankind he had never thought that he might benefit them also and thus swell with theirs his sum of pleasure. His first aim must be to render mankind happy; and now he began to have a dim idea of the import of warring parties which so abused each other. This was the secret of the contest, the master-spring; which of the two could do most good to the people; which best knew how to do it? He has an interview with Salinguerra, but leaves him more perplexed than before. He strays about the streets, looking at the misery that war has wrought, "to serve," as he says, "Taurello's ends." He forgets that it is equally to serve Azzo's or St. Boniface's. He stands among the throng about the Veronese carroch, and being recognized as a minstrel, is called upon to sing a song of Sordello's. Then he rejoices that this noble gift is his, and having sung, turns to a youth beside him, to whom he declares his name. The youth is Palma in disguise, and she leads him away from the place.

Taurello has seen the envoys of Emperor and Pope, and now he sits alone. On the wall of the chamber the green and yellow colors of Romano flank the two-headed eagle of the Empire; on the table lie the imperial rescript and badge which may make him the Vicar of Frederick in Northern Italy. But his thoughts are strangely drawn to Sordello, the last, as he is the first servant of Romano. How great the contrast! The minstrel's thirty years spent in doing nothing, this day's journey their greatest event; how lean and old they have left him, how awkward and ill at ease he looks; while Salinguerra, sixty years old, after a life spent in camp and court, with Popes and Emperors, is quick, graceful, splendid. Beside the Kaiser's rescript lies a letter from Ecelin, emphasizing his withdrawal from active life. Shall he fill Romano's place, and reign as the Emperor's Vicar?

He recalls his past life; how, when yet a boy, he had been robbed of his promised bride by St. Boniface's father, who had wedded her to Azzo of Este. He had then betaken himself to Sicily and the court of Henry of Swabia, whence he afterwards returned, bringing with him a fair southern bride, Retrude, of the imperial Hohenstaufen line, for whom he built a palace and prepared broad gardens more noble than any Ferrara could display; and when his son was born to him, men said that he would visit Mantua and assert his power there also. And now the Guelfs, fearful of losing place, rise in arms, and the Ghibelline quarter of the city was fired in a fray in which Ecelin had endeavored to put down the insurrection. Taurello then lost wife and child, and became henceforth fully absorbed in the fortunes of Romano, whom he supports, aided by Adelaide. His course is quite incomprehensible to Henry, as to his brother Philip, for they value Salinguerra far higher than his lord. Otto IV., seeing Ecelin harsh and unready, Taurello facile and sparkling, concludes that his predecessors' judgments have been influenced by outside show, and so fixes his choice upon the former.

Such is Salinguerra, who, with no thought of graces, took them as they came ; learned to speak Greek, because Greeks are hard to hold to contracts ; learned Arabic, because that helped him to master astrology, in which he assisted Adelaide, who relied for much of her power on magic ; controlled Frederick ;

patronized art; sang, played upon the lute, and was a mighty warrior in battle.

Salinguerra, who wished to look into the minds of men that he might learn their purposes and capabilities, displayed himself so far as was needful to make men display themselves.

Sordello cared to know men merely that he might display himself, and valued them only as they drew out or expressed that self in him.

As time passed on, men noticed that whenever Taurello was absent the power of Romano waned, nor could he be prevailed upon always to recall his adviser; his wife was his chief support, and when she died destruction threatened. Then Taurello once more assumed his old part, restored things by a touch, and struck Este down. Men remembered now the old hate he bore to Azzo, which of late had been prudently concealed, for not only Azzo's fall, but the ruin of the whole House of Este was what he desired.

He stands thoughtful in the window, and there rises up before him that whole night of fire and blood, when all he loved was lost, and he determines that Ecelin, whose wife and child were saved, shall help him to revenge. He can be Vicar if he choose; but to what end? His life must wear itself out in the roar and foam of adventure, nor will any trace of him remain. Fate has ordained that he shall make others powerful, not himself, nor can he bear to thrust Ecelin's children from their father's place.

Sordello and Palma stand together by an extinguished watch-fire; he entreats her to tell him how to play a man's part in the world; to show him if somehow good may be the final goal behind all the ill he sees; shall he believe in Salinguerra, who seems to be all that Sordello should be? But he does so many deeds of violence; do the Guelfs commit such acts also? And Palma shows him that the Guelfs are indeed no more just or gentle. Then he feels that since both parties are so evil in what they do, he is rather worthy of praise than blame for having done nothing, since, if he has accomplished no good, at least he has wrought no ill. And he fancies that there may be a third cause, which it is left to him to discover. Here a bystander bids him take as the subject of a ballad the famous Crescentius. Sordello has never heard of him, and the speaker, who was once a friar, goes on to tell him how that man had defied both Pope and Emperor, had been called Roman Consul, had trusted the people, and wished to restore the vanished Republic. Pope and Emperor combined against him, and he was crucified in the Forum. Sordello is called upon to sing to the people a song of Rome.

And in truth Rome seemed to him to be the one point of light that was to illuminate the world; all other cities but strove to resemble it; Guelf and Ghibelline sought, not to change, but to possess it; then let Rome advance! It was Rome as she seemed to the ignorant Sordello, and Rome was the cause he longed to uphold: the ancient Rome, the Rome of the Civil Law, of the Capitol, of St. Angelo; where the new is brought into harmony with the old, the temporal with the spiritual; law, order, religion, all from the type of that power that shall give its rights unto mankind.

"Let us have Rome again!" cries Sordello. "I am the one fated to rebuild it; such a future is the justification of such a past!" And full of this thought he rushes out to make it living among the people, to let their facts complete his dream.

BOOK V.

BUT the evening sees Sordello in another mood. His dream of Rome without an Emperor has faded. The people whom he has seen, drunken, ignorant, brutal, are scarcely the ideal citizens of his ideal city. Yet he should remember how great of old was the labor of building the Roman state; how mankind has toiled upward from the cave-dwellers to the workers in brick and stone. How use came first, and how art then followed. The work moved on step by step; there was no possibility of overleaping details and gaining the full glory at a bound, when every change in building-materials exacted an architect and an age. The men to whom a maple log was a luxury hardly cared for priceless Mauritanian tables.[1]

[1] Citrus-wood tables sent from Northern Africa brought fabulous prices in the luxurious days of Rome.

"Better," you say, "to merge all common workmen in the master, all epochs in one." Then indeed the sudden city might bask in the daylight, but its citizens would be quite incapable of comprehending or enjoying the privileges that had fallen to their lot.

"Enough of Rome," thinks Sordello. "Fate has added another to the list of beautiful things that Sordello cannot do."

Thus sitting, lonely and despondent, he hears within his heart a voice that speaks: "God, Sordello, has given to man two sights — one of the perfected plan of time, one of the moment's work; what have you lost save the hope of taking that supreme step, the knowledge of which was vouchsafed to you, that you might have courage to take your own step, and to abide by that, leaving the end to hope? All that is gone is the glory that crowns the labor, and which, could you thus speedily compass, you were God, not man. The first step is still yours to take, and you are to learn this truth, that mankind can accomplish more than any individual man; but there must be some one to take the first step. There is no perfect poet, for one excels in strength, and one in grace. So it is in the world at large. Are you the first to give a definite form to the many? Was there not, centuries ago, one who devised an apparition in the midst of that loose, perpetual unrest? A sudden, splendid flower who drew all things to himself, the child of joyous life, the embodiment of strength; — Charlemagne has lived. So strong and grand and calm, he seems unfeeling in his superb confidence and content. He formed of the multitude one magnificent body; is it the province of Hildebrand[1] to vitalize that body with a soul? Is the State strength, and the Church knowledge? For three hundred years the two powers have appeared to touch each other; the great

[1] Hildebrand, or Gregory VII., one of the most famous of the Popes. He enforced the celibacy of the clergy, and attempted to deprive laymen of all part in investing the clergy with their offices. He lived in the latter part of the eleventh century. Contemporary and opponent of the Emperor Henry IV.

Cæsars bear up the Crowns,[1] the iron of Aix, the silver of Milan, and the gold of Rome; the great Popes lift up the Keys. But how do the great and small unite? The Crusaders seek to create strength by other aid than strength alone; a spiritual force is behind them; it is a safe plan; as also is that of the League, which opposes force by force; while from the preaching of the clergy may come the possibility of superseding strength. Who, strong in being feeling yet unfeeling too, shall bring in the next age? No, Sordello believes Hildebrand's task is not yet accomplished; there is still work for him to do. In thought he wrenches asunder the scaffold of Charles; but the work starts back, and he feels that he can only confirm and better, not destroy; that strength and knowledge

[1] The crown of the German kingdom taken at Aachen, of Lombardy at Milan, of the Empire at Rome. They were said to be respectively of silver, iron, and gold. Not quite in the order of the text. The terms were probably employed symbolically, as indicating the estimation in which each was held at that time.

must work together; that the warrior and the poet should no longer be dissevered in him, and since he is ambitious of remodeling the world, let him go to Salinguerra, and secure his aid to keep the Guelfs in power."

He finds Taurello and Palma together; he has his chance at last, and he makes the most of it. But after all his rhetoric avails only to show that he would turn Salinguerra to the papal side; that the God of Goito has dwindled into a Guelfic partisan; and his old fault recurs: he cannot help looking at himself while he is speaking, and wondering how his hearers are impressed, as he shows the great chief how necessary it is that Lombardy should get rid of her barons. Meanwhile Taurello, famed for tact, a man who, careless of phrases, never lacked the right one, looked as if all were as it should be, and he were interested in every point. His only answer is, "Does poetry turn hair white sooner than politics?"

Then the bitter truth flashes upon Sordello that fancies have so weakened his power, that he no longer possesses earnestness, nor the wish to work, nor yet the power to express how urgent is the need of working. He sees the base years drag on into the future, while he writes many poems, no doubt, and will be mourned when dead as one whose best survives him. Better tear out the heart of the truth at once! Once more he begins to speak; the bells of the carrochs sound from the square below; Taurello lifts the imperial badge, and smilingly asks Palma if this will satisfy her; if he shall set Boniface free, submit their strength to the Pope's knowledge, and bestow the Emperor's badge upon Azzo. And, laughing, he wonders who will hereafter censure the minstrel for lack of wisdom; surely this speech would have been greatly preferable to the bull-fight he had lately been forced to witness.

But contempt saved what vanity had wellnigh destroyed, and Sordello now found words to speak out his thoughts; and he closes with the bitter expression of his despair that he must not only resign to Taurello the post he had longed to fill, but must see the baron scorn to take the place. Then the old Goito days return once more; he is Apollo and knows that the minstrel is indeed a king, and that if he fail of asserting his proper royalty, it is not because the royalty is lacking, but that he has been thrust aside as inexpert to fill the poet's throne. He has seen too late that kingship does not lie in the forms he would imitate; these he could but copy. Include the multitude, and let it include you in turn; so shall you fill your place, to make way in another age for yet another sovereign. Before song, deeds made up the world, but thought is the soul of action, and the poet presents to us the masque of life, and shows its varied forms, and allots to each its praise or blame. The poet turns ends attained to means, and from the old structures he erects the new, as Venice plunders every clime to make her Duomo splendid. To the Guelfic cause, which he believes the People's, he would win Salinguerra, who, long past surprise, turns to Palma, and says briefly, "You love him, and you know your father's will, who would, by giving up much of his territory, procure from the Pope peace for his two sons. And so would end all my hopes! Shall they so end, or shall I try my fortune? Nay, the place is for the young and not for me. If you were Ecelin!—but stay—this youth has flattered me as I have not been flattered this many a day. A little help might make a leader of him." And turning he flings upon Sordello's neck the Emperor's badge.

"You are Romano's head, and you shall have Palma for your spouse!"

Then as they gazed into each other's eyes a truth grew up between them; sire and son sat by each other, while Palma recounted the tale she had heard from Adelaide's dying lips, and they learned that on that awful night of fire and slaughter Retrude, Salinguerra's wife, had been rescued with her infant, and borne to Goito, where she

shortly after died, and was buried beneath the font where Sordello so oft had rested. Her son was hidden away by Adelaide, and feigned an archer's child, lest Taurello, having him to live for, should come into his true place, and overtop her husband.

Hardly able to grasp the truth, Salinguerra talks wildly of all he will do for his son, so late known to him, until Palma takes his arms from Sordello's neck, and leads him from the room. Still he talks on of politics with Palma, when she turns him from that subject to tell him how all men love the poet, while Taurello drinks in every word, and foretells great glory to Romano when Palma and Sordello shall be united. Strong they shall be, he declares, to overthrow Hildebrand and build up Charles, but adding to strength knowledge.

Suddenly a sound comes to them, which silences speech. "'T is his own footstep, his summons!" and they stagger quickly up the stair.

BOOK VI.

IT was a thought of Eglamor's that man shrinks into nothingness when matched with the symbols of immensity, and must quail before a quiet sea or sky. And as the evening sank low, and only one spot of light gleamed upon the opposite river, something in Sordello's mood seemed to confirm its speciousness. So he sat, until roused by the din of the city, while memory brought all his own life in review before him, a life where each change seemed to him to have been right, until, viewing it in the light of present knowledge, he could see how it had checked some other. The true way seemed to be formed of all ways, many moods of the one mind, tokens of an existence which needed but some outer influence, some soul above his soul to lift it, as the moon stirs the depths of ocean. But no moon of love arose in his sky, and thus his sensitiveness had grown or dwindled at caprice, and was spilt in showers of foam, never gathered up into one mighty wave encompassing the earth. Others, less than he, had yet some core within, that, yielding to some moon, fulfilled a certain purpose in the world.

To every one who lives there must be some fruit of life, to each in his own degree; to every one there must be some point toward which he tends; spirits, compressing all they know of beauty into one star of glory, dream that one day it will bestow upon them some gleams of its own splendor. Whether it be beauty that they crave, or knowledge, whether it be love or hate, they yet pursue something above them, something beyond their present existence. Not that love like Palma's or hate like Salinguerra's would be equal to swaying all Sordello. Why doubt that there must be somewhere love to match his strength, some moon to be meet for his sea? Why fear, since he has known the Good, that he shall not some day know the Best? Ah, but the Best eludes us; we had hoped for men far beyond those we see about us, and we may be foolish, seeing a good, to argue a best beyond. Is an external power needed? May he not be ordained a law unto himself? If laws are veiled in mercy to those who cannot strive unless some embodied want lure them on! A stronger vision could endure the bodiless want, nor would it mistake a bauble for a truth. The People were himself, and was he less impelled by pity to alter the discrepancies in their position than if a sickly part were abstracted from a sound whole, and palmed off upon him as alien suffering? Proud to forsake himself, shall he aid the Guelfs? No, all is himself, and all service rates alike, not serving one by destroying another, but all in time. "Put by the picturesque achievements for the present, and do the daily, common tasks." The People urge their claims, and he now realizes how much easier it is to do some one great act, to soften signal horrors, than by constant, vast and hidden toil to assuage constant, vast and hidden suffering. Now the People are in need of help, and how small the service that he can render, ever could have rendered! Let youth be aware that it has surprised one serviceable truth; can it use it, and turn to seize a fresh prey? Nay, it takes a lifetime to bring this within the comprehension of the crowd, and ere that is done the captor sees a crowd of other truths yet nobler, which he might learn had he as many lives. And he recalls the story of many a bard who has sunken below manhood in grasping at the divine.

"Yet to begin merits a crown! Truth must be casual truth, nor is it likely that the whole truth, which, if rightly apprehended, had sent the world upon its proper pathway, has ever been at one time in the world. One must be content with the chance sparkles now and then struck out." Now was the moment for Sordello's gleam, wretched though it was. He would dash the Cæsar's badge to the ground, perhaps persuade Taurello to turn Frederick from his purpose; at least he can bear witness to his own belief. But first let him consider; were that little truly service? "In the end, no doubt, but in the time between? Would that it were as easy to see what each day's fraction of work should be, as to comprehend what befits the sum of life!"

Sordello never doubts that he should aid the Guelfs, but to do this various natures must be controlled, and moved with reference to future ends; old loves and hates, the sympathy or aversion of the Present must be put aside for the sake of so feeble a Future. For slightest cause must men be saved if they will aid the Papal party, for slightest cause destroyed if they oppose it. Shall he ruin many good purposes for the sake of one? Spoil a good work half done for one just begun? Rise one step with the People to sink one? Evil is everywhere made beautiful; shall Beauty then be thrust aside that we may be rid of Evil? Is not Evil, after all, as natural a result as Good?

Pass over the struggles of trees and flowers with the seasons, the miserable strife among beasts, care only for man, and we see that it is the sorrow caused by the ills he suffers that charms one's sympathy; were he free from sorrow he were free from you. Joy itself is but the overcoming of obstacles, the making the privileges of the few the possession of the many. The quiet perfections of Goito had wearied him, and it is by triumphing over difficulties that men win salvation; the view of life is disclosed by degrees, as we climb the mountain-sides; scaling height after height, and piercing veil after misty veil, we take fresh courage; in the soul is formed the idea of that Whole, which we must seek by Parts; had the Whole been ours at first what enjoyment could have been ours of gradual gains? The time that seems so short to include all the Parts were more than enough to exhaust the Whole were it once attained, and all that we should have gained would be leave to look, not leave to do. To look beneath is soon enjoyed, but to one who looks above, death comes before a tithe of life has been tasted. Live first, Sordello! die then soon enough! Give to body and spirit their first right, the right to life, and feel that you are able to extort joy from sorrow, and gold from clods, which to all but you are clods only, and would have remained forever such, had you not lighted for them your refining fires.

It had been better if you had but secured an ampler treasure! They crave, as it is, a share that ruins you, and will not save them. Why, for the sake of sympathy, should you renounce what delights you, and cannot benefit them? Would all reach joy? The road is one for all, but the times of journeying are many; hinder no soul that in the general march has the earlier start; all come at length to the same point. Help on the crowd's *Then*, but remember how this badge would make your *Now* more joyous.

As he mused, his capacity for action seemed to grow to giant size compared with the impotence of the world at large to profit by the sacrifice of his happiness. Shall he make nothing of his life because it is so brief? Nay, rather, for that very reason make more of it! Leave virtue untried, and grasp the delights of sin, and if time condemn, Sordello will have slipped away to the quiet of Goito.

The active few can cope with the many; be active, then! And even if the multitude suffer somewhat, 't is but one pang to the brimming bowl of pleasure. Does Fate really destine him to live in the Eternal City? To live! It is the cry of Sordello's heart, to live once before he dies! Helps and hinderances he disregards if only he may live, live now, not wait for some transcendent future. Perhaps, after death, a grander glory may await his soul, but how to be enjoyed he cannot tell. Fate is exhaustless for him, but does she bid him grasp what the present brings or wait for future splendors? It were absurd to slight the present for the hereafter. Here is the crowd which he is willing to spend his life in serving, if only he may serve it. If not, why require more of him?

"I will take the gift," he cries, "nor will I falter in my journey, nor decry life and its delights. I will praise the World, though it be, as you declare, but the anteroom to a palace; shall I assume the airs of a palace before its doors are open to me? Shall I, in the enjoyment of future bliss, regret that I disdained what the present offers?

"Let me, then, have stronger hands and feet, but for the present no wings. And yet this cup, which I would drain even to the dregs, has been so often dashed aside; I have so often had glimpses of a better life, hidden by this, a life fearlessly sought by martyr, champion, and sage. Let me but see that, and I too am glad to die. Let that which masters life but show itself! But since truth appears so various, and every circle has its own law, how can one discern abstract right?" And so for the moment all qualities of good and evil seemed to Sordello but moods of this world, not made to bind Eternity and Mind.

Then suddenly he felt himself alone, out of time and the world. What had caused all his past despair? Just this. Soul being thrust upon matter, joy comes when so much soul is wreaked in time on matter, but if the soul raise matter beyond what was intended, and so prevent the performance of actions, sorrow is the result. The infinite soul tries to instruct the body as to its capabilities, and in yearning after perfection it loses the opportunities it might enjoy; till, worn out with efforts to attain what is beyond its grasp, leaving virtue and beauty unattained, the soul seeks to show that these qualities belong to time alone, and that the body may turn ill to good, and reap joy where sorrow was meant to grow. Then the body perishes under what should have been a blessing, leaving the soul in dismay. Can one soul never behold all that is, the great Before and After, and the small Now? But where shall we find the supreme Love that shall show the course that soul must travel? Here is a soul upon which Nature has exhausted all her resources, from tree and flower to mankind at large. Shall he save that or not?

Ah, Sordello, what need there is of a power so far above you that you cannot regard it as a rival! Of a Power, the representative of nature, the same in authority but different in communication, which should claim a course clear as Human, though hidden as Divine!

What has Sordello found! Or can his spirit go the mighty round to end where Eglamor began? As says the old fable, that two eagles flew two different ways about the earth, and where they met men set the temple of Jove.

Whose step is first that rushes up the stair? It is Salinguerra's, though sheathed in mail. They enter, and behold Sordello dead, beneath his feet the badge, and in his eyes a look of triumph, like that of some spent swimmer, who sees in his despair help coming from above; for he has trampled upon what seemed to him a temptation to evil, the temptation to accept a life lower than his ideal, and has perished in the struggle, but the prize of victory is his.

Alas, Sordello, whom they laid in the old font-tomb at Goito at his mother's side!

Time passes, and young Ecelin comes to fill the first place in Lombardy. Strange that Sordello's inability to shut out rivals from the stage, an inability due to his fatal disbelief in the possibility of accomplishing anything, thrust the two sons of Romano into Taurello's guardianship, and enabled the wretched pair to demonstrate that wherever there is the will to do, something can always be done, whether for good or ill. And so they plagued the world, till men rose up and slew them.

The chronicles of Mantua tell how Sordello, Prince Visconti, saved that city and elsewhere distinguished himself greatly; that he was famous as a minstrel and fortunate as a lover; he was praised for the very things he never did and never could have done.

For what he should have been, what he might have been and would not, we suffer to this day. The best chance that there was for humanity Ecelin destroyed before Dante could come, and for the sake of the suffering world dared boldly to take the step Sordello spurned. Dante did much, Sordello's chance was lost forever.

Had he dared take that step alone, he had compassed Apollo. It was a chance, he would have come to him rather than go to it.

Like one who would gladly sleep at home, while supposed to be fighting or singing abroad, he valued the few real things he had achieved mainly because he had thus learned that they are valueless and need never be done again.

Had Sordello but boldly embraced the chance then offered to him, men would have plucked the apples of Hesperides, and praising the benefits that he bestowed, have given him all that he wished to appear, but hardly desired to be.

After all a life such as his is but a sorry farce. Can we say nothing better of him than this?

In the bright summer morning while the lark sings, mounting heavenward, above the castle-walls, a merry boy brushes the dew from the grass as he passes, and glad at heart he sings — his song one fragment of the old Goito lay, that spoke the praise of Elys. Sleep and forget, Sordello!

A STUDY OF THE CHARACTER OF SORDELLO.

You say, "Since so it is, good-bye,
  Sweet life, high hope; but whatsoe'er
May be, or must, no tongue shall dare
  To tell, 'The Lombard feared to die!'"
                    ARTHUR HUGH CLOUGH.

A STUDY OF THE CHARACTER OF SORDELLO.

Mr. Browning tells us that the story of Sordello is the history of the development of a soul.

It would seem to be, in some respects, the story of a soul whose complete and harmonious development has been thwarted by the circumstances amid which it finds itself; cut off by a lonely life from the educating influences of the outside world and from that correction of individual views that comes from contact with one's fellows.

His is a soul whose noblest aspirations are hindered by a certain self-consciousness from which it can never escape; a soul too weak and inexperienced to control circumstances, too willful to follow, but not ardent enough to lead; too unformed in judgment of men and of affairs, and too deficient in political insight to discover the better way; too true and noble to accept what it believes to be the worse.

He is the son of a brave and accomplished mediæval chieftain, who has been nurtured in camps and courts, and who, like so many of his contemporaries, is statesman, courtier, warrior, and minstrel in one; his mother is of that wondrous Hohenstaufen House, in which great mental gifts seem to have been a birthright. But Sordello, with a soul full of lofty ambitions, grows up in the belief that he is an archer's son, who is held to have attained high honor when he has become his lady's chosen minstrel.

His boyhood and youth are passed in a romantic castle, situated in a solitary spot, among the mountains, surrounded by woods and marshes, in the company of a few objects of semi-classic art, and with trees and flowers, animals and birds for his play-fellows, while over him bends the blue Italian sky.

Human companionship he has none; his

heart swells with longing to enter into the life of everything about him; plant and animal gain a certain spiritual life from him, but at the expense of too great self-effacement on his part. The figures that are most like humanity are the painted warriors on the arras, and these, too, in his fancies, he bids live and act.

All the castle is free to him, save the northern chambers, and so, too, are the woods and fields about it; of anything of the outer world he has but two brief glimpses: one, when accidentally penetrating into the forbidden apartments, he encounters the Ladye of the castle and a fair maiden, who sits beside her; one, when Ecelin, the master of the house, comes to visit his wife and daughter, and Sordello watches his archer train wind slowly in and out among the vines, and recognizes even then that there may be a tie of kinship between the humble house-leek on the roof and the proud baron in his ringing mail.

A few chance words spoken by the bowmen, a hint now and then from the foreign serving-women about him, are all the reports that come to him from the outside life of the world.

Time passes in vague dreams and aimless fantasies; unconscious himself of the want, he stands in need of some power outside of and beyond himself, some overmastering purpose that shall show to him some goal towards which to strive. As he grows older he ceases to make trees and flowers his comrades, their places are filled by human images, or rather by certain personified essential qualities of humanity, as strength, grace, wisdom; these qualities are gradually combined in his mind until they are reduced to a few, which are in their turn resolved into one grand personality, to which he longs to give a name.

Who is this type of all wise and heroic qualities? Is it the Cæsar? Or does he dwell in such ineffable greatness, so remote from the life of the multitude, that no touch of emotion can come to him from the crowd of unhappy men and women who are perishing for lack of help?

Or is it perhaps the minstrel, who rules the world by song?

Is it possible that it may one day be his destiny to combine the two, to act and to sing, to be both Cæsar and Apollo?

But there is in Sordello's spiritual life one fatal defect, a certain self-consciousness, that will one day be his ruin; he never ceases to question what men will think about him, how his deeds and words are regarded by the world. Even when, in his dreams, he has trampled all his foes beneath his feet and only admiring worshipers remain; when in his heart he has taken the proud resolve that only his lord's fair daughter, who has hitherto disdained all suitors, shall be his future bride, the Daphne to his Apollo; — even then he cannot refrain from looking forward to the time when the whole world shall see and envy him her love, and when great cities shall bow down before him in reverence for his fame.

That world with which he has never measured himself, whose stern criticism he has never felt, for conflict with which he has never yet braced heart and soul, is waiting, he believes, but for his coming to hail him for its king!

Then comes the day which brings him before his wished-for public, the day which makes him Palma's minstrel. His triumph for the moment is complete, but he soon ceases to be content with his position. He cares more for the effect his song produces, than he does for the song itself, and he becomes weary of the labor which the work requires. He falls into conventional ways, and is satisfied with laurels too lightly won. At length he sickens of popular applause, and withdraws for a time from public view, that he may devote himself to the task of elaborating a more perfect instrument of expression. He desires to make the Italian as suitable for poetic use as the more polished Langue d'Oc; he would sing in the speech of the people, and so become more fully the people's poet. And he has a momentary success. But he fails to thoroughly embody in words the fervid perceptions which offer themselves, they are too subtle and evanescent to be intellectually apprehended, or expressed. Up to this moment he has felt only, he has not yet thought. The Mantuans care little for his efforts; they prefer to walk in trodden paths, and he abandons his language, wrought with so much care, takes up the old measures and the common themes, and sings the exploits of a crusading hero. Even now his full meaning is missed, and weary of being perpetually misunderstood, Sordello once more withdraws from public life.

He feels two natures struggling within him, man and poet: the man craves action and life in the world; the poet longs for solitude and song; he cannot reconcile the two.

"Take things as they are," say the Mantuans; "suit yourself to the ordinary ways of life." He tries and fails again.

Then Taurello comes to Mantua, and as Palma's minstrel it is Sordello's duty to bid him welcome; but inspiration fails him, and he flees to Goito, where nature soothes his grief, and calms his troubled soul. His mind sleeps, and he knows that it does so.

Is it really true that his youth can never return, that he has forfeited all hopes of love and power and fame? Must all aspirations be abandoned forever? He feels that even the crowd of common men have this advantage over him, that they are endowed with a personality distinct from what they see, while he is perpetually driven to blend himself with all that he beholds. Is it his fate to be forever thrust aside, the spectator of joys to which he can never attain? Rather seize any happiness that offers! — and with the thought comes a message bidding him return to Mantua. And here love greets him while Palma smiles, and whispers at once of her love for him for whom she has so long waited, and of the political schemes in which she seeks his aid.

Of late Sordello's soul has been inspired with a new and more unselfish purpose, the wish to help mankind. He pities the sufferings of the multitude, and longs to aid. He knows not by what means his ends are to be attained, whether political or social. He sees the horrors of the conflict between Guelf and Ghibelline, but he feels sure that there must be some choice between them, that the great question is, which can most effectually help the people. He talks with Salinguerra, he listens to Palma, and implores her to teach him to play a man's part in the world, and, wandering through the streets ravaged by war, he hears from a bystander in the market-place the story of Crescentius, as it appears encircled with the mythic glories of the past; the legend of the Tribune, who would have built up a Rome without a Pope and without an Emperor.

This, Sordello fancies, may be his destined work. To rebuild Rome! But it must be the Rome of the People, and he finds that the people as they are, down-trodden, brutal, ignorant, are not fit to be the denizens of his ideal city. It behooves him now to remember how great was the work to found the Rome of old; to remember how men have worked their way upward from the cave-dwellers to the architects of palaces and temples; that every succeeding step has been taken with weariness and toil; that the many can accomplish more than any one, but that there must always be the one man to take the first step, to lead the way, it may be to perish in so doing. That the work moves on by slow degrees, helped by many hands. If all could be instantly caught up to the standpoint of one greatest soul, if all epochs could be merged in one, the sudden city would glitter in splendor in the noonday sun, but its citizens would be unable either to comprehend or enjoy its delights.

And so he puts that dream by. Then he seems to hear a voice within him saying that God has vouchsafed to man two sights: one of the future with its completed work, that perfect ideal which is to be one day the actual; one of the daily tasks that must be wrought to make that work complete; the glimpse of the first should encourage us to undertake the second, to compass both is beyond the lot of mortal. Each must work for all; each has his share, however small, to contribute; the step that each man takes helps on the universal march.

But Sordello is not the first who has sought to form mankind into a definite shape — to make of Humanity an organic whole. Centuries before there had blossomed a splendid flower that had drawn all things into itself; Charles the Great had lived, an embodiment of joyous, active, fruitful life, incarnate strength. Was it the part of Hildebrand to spiritualize this body? Does the Empire represent strength and the Church knowledge? Has either accomplished all that it might have done? The League opposes force by force; were it not better to listen to the voice of the gentle friar who is preaching of peace? Can knowledge render strength needless? Is the work of Hildebrand to supersede the work of Charles? Sordello believes so, and determines to overthrow the latter. He ponders long, and sees that the task is beyond his power, the work is too strong to be destroyed, the State is needful to man; strength must be combined with knowledge, Cæsar and Apollo, knight and minstrel, must strive together to the same end.

He seeks Salinguerra to convert him to Guelfic politics, and entreat his aid to benefit the world. There is a strange mixture of tragedy and comedy in the scene between Taurello and his unknown son, between the all-accomplished cavalier to whom all graces come unsought, and the poet, old before his time, ignorant of the world, without tact, and possessed by an idea, which yet does not so thoroughly possess him as to render him oblivious of self and careless of what others may think or say of him.

He tells the fiery Ghibelline, whose life

has been blasted by Guelfic hate, that the Pope's cause is the cause of humanity; he tells the haughty noble that the one thing that Lombardy most needs is to be rid of her barons!

Suddenly he realizes the absurdity of the situation; — the god of Goito sunken into a partisan of the Guelfs! But the touch of playful sarcasm which Taurello cannot resist rouses Sordello at last to something really living, and he bursts forth into a splendid eulogium of the rank and functions of the poet, and the scene ends with the conferring of the viceroyalty upon him by Salinguerra, and the disclosure by Palma of the true relations in which the two stand to each other. Then she withdraws the bewildered father from the room, and Sordello is left to meditate upon his position, and determine upon his future course.

If he accept the viceroyalty he will have all of its best that life can give him, and he longs for the joys of life. Why should he put off the enjoyment of happiness to another world, to a future state in which he may reproach himself that he had undervalued the gifts of the present? If this world be indeed but the ante-chamber of a palace, so be it; but why assume, as yet, the airs of the palace? Never for the sake of his own pleasure will he deprive any man of his rights; all paths lead to the same goal, the road is free to all, and all men shall certainly arrive at last at the longed-for destination.

But it may well be that some shall reach the end toward which they toil earlier than others because they have the advantage in the start.

But is there, after all, as some have said, anything nobler to be attained than earthly joy?

If that indeed be so, for that supreme happiness he will gladly forego all present delights.

But what is the true path into which the loftiest aspirations should lead his steps? What is the cause of truth and duty and God?

He had believed it possible for him to find a third cause to which to consecrate his powers, the cause of the people, but it seems to him now that from the people themselves he can look for but little assistance; the third cause is not yet, at least, self-supporting, it cannot stand alone. He believes that it must be committed to the guardianship of one of the two parties which seem to divide the world between them, that he must range himself with either Guelf or Ghibelline.

And he believes, too, that the choice lies with the Guelfs. Without experience, prone to theorize with but a slight comprehension of facts as a basis, he decides that the world must be saved through knowledge, and that this knowledge is to be found in the Church alone.

He makes, as he thinks, the choice between Charles and Hildebrand; had he comprehended the work of the first Teutonic Emperor, he had not so believed; had he known anything of the Hohenstaufen in whose reign he lived, he would never have so fatally misjudged.

But in his frame of mind the imperial viceroyalty comes to him in the guise of a temptation to abandon his convictions of right, and for once in his life Sordello gathers up all his forces for one mighty effort, one great struggle to overcome. And the effort is in itself a triumph. He flings the Cæsar's badge upon the ground, and tramples beneath his feet its glittering lure. Action is forbidden him; his only privilege is to renounce, and when he resolutely thrusts behind him all the joys of earth, death opens to him in mercy the gates of Heaven. He has won a spiritual victory and the reward of all efforts to overcome self, and to grasp a noble ideal is his.

> "'T is better to have fought, and lost,
> Than never to have fought at all!"

But for his failures in courage, in faith and judgment, the world, alas! must suffer.

He could not see that, for good or for evil, something can always be done, if the fixed will to do exist; that his own judgment in political affairs was too devoid of experience to be of any value, and that in taking up the work which was placed at his disposal he would have secured an unrivaled opportunity to aid the suffering, and relieve the oppressed.

His inexperience of the world, his incapacity to forget himself, his scorn of gradual progress toward the desired end, joined to Palma's inability to inspire him with her own spirit, all led him astray.

As it seemed to him, the viceroyalty was a temptation, and he justly spurned it, but then came in his place the sons of Romano, and made the land a hell.

The language he had abandoned, Dante, a century later, made an unsurpassed vehicle, not only of the most fervid perception, but of the profoundest thought. The political views he rejected were the life of Dante's soul, as deeply felt and as sincerely cherished as his religion. But he combined strength and knowledge; he was Cæsar and

Apollo, Man and Poet in one. And he did much. " Sordello's chance," says Mr. Browning, " was gone."

But Dante never forgot that Sordello had taken one of those first steps which cost, albeit he had not the faith or persistence to continue in the path upon which he had entered. The future generations gave to the Sordello of legend all the worldly success which he had so vainly longed for, and fancied him triumphant as warrior, statesman, and lover; but his truest glory is, that, first of northern Italians, he strove to sing to the people in their own tongue, that he took the first step upon that Sacred Way over which Dante marched in triumph.

On the Mount of Purgatory, gracious and calm, but lonely as on earth, the Mantuan Sordello greets the Mantuan Virgil, his immortal countryman, and gives a kindly welcome to the mighty Tuscan, who is destined so grandly to fulfill what had been to the Troubadour aspirations only.

And on the sunny slopes of Mount Parnassus, where the divine Apollo sits, surrounded by his disciples, there, among the greatest poets of the world, has Raphael placed Sordello.

The lofty poet, whose vision penetrated into the darkest abysses and the most radiant splendors of the other world, a sorrowful exile from his native city, unites with the gentle, happy painter in rendering immortal the name of one whose earthly life had seemed to himself a failure, whose one supreme success was the renunciation of all the joys of earth and even of life itself.

Robert Browning's Works.

That Mr. Browning is the strongest man who now writes English poetry — the strongest who has written since Milton died — no sane man will deny. — F. J. FURNIVALL.

Poems and Dramas. In two volumes. 16mo, $3.00.

Sordello, Strafford, Christmas Eve, and Easter Day. 16mo, $1.50.

Dramatis Personæ. 16mo, $1.50.

Men and Women. 16mo, $1.50.

The Ring and the Book. In two volumes. 16mo, $3.00.

Balaustion's Adventure. 16mo, $1.50.

Fifine at the Fair. Prince Hohensteil Schwangau and Hervé Riel. 16mo, $1.50.

Red Cotton Night-Cap Country; or, Turf and Towers. 16mo, $1.50.

The Inn Album. 16mo, $1.50.

Pacchiarotto and Other Poems. 16mo, $1.50.

Agamemnon, La Saisiaz, Two Poets of Croisic, Pauline, and Dramatic Idyls (First and Second Series). 16mo, $1.50.

Jocoseria. 16mo, $1.00.

Ferishtah's Fancies. 16mo, $1.00.

Favorite Poems. In "Modern Classics," No. 12. 32mo, orange edges, 75 cents. *School Edition*, 40 cents.

Works. New Edition. In eight volumes. Crown 8vo, gilt top, $13.00; half calf, $22.50. (*Sold only in sets.*)

Jocoseria. Uniform with New Edition of Works. Crown 8vo, gilt top, $1.00.

Ferishtah's Fancies. Uniform with the above. Crown 8vo, gilt top, $1.00.

In the case of Robert Browning we find an originality which, of itself, is one of the strongest imaginable claims upon respect, and one of the greatest imaginable attractions. We rejoice in the vigor and self-reliance of such a minstrel: we honor the manliness of his muse. Write what he will, and how he will, no lover of poetry, or student of language, can fail to enjoy and profit by his verse. — *New York Times.*

Whilst he stands among the foremost of living poets, his wealth of thought, his bold and strong imagination, his quaint fancy and subtle humor, are clothed in a rich diction, so involved, and at times so obscure, that to read him is working a mine to obtain treasures such as he alone has to bestow, and that fully reward the toil, however great. — *Boston Transcript.*

⁎ For sale by all Booksellers. Sent by mail, post-paid, on receipt of price by the Publishers,

HOUGHTON, MIFFLIN & CO.
BOSTON AND NEW YORK.

www.ingramcontent.com/pod-product-compliance
Lightning Source LLC
Chambersburg PA
CBHW030333170426
43202CB00010B/1115